Strange Williamsburg Hill

Larry Wilson

Copyright © 2020 Larry Wilson
First Edition: December 2020
All rights reserved.
ISBN-13: 978-1-7334631-3-3

ACKNOWLEDGEMENTS

To my family, friends, and colleagues for their patience during the completion of the writing of this book. A special thank you to Carl Jones for sharing his haunting experience, for his valued friendship and for the work he does as a respected and trusted colleague in the field of paranormal investigation.

Contents

	Acknowledgements
7	Dedication
8	From the Author
9	Prologue
13	**The Hill**
13	History
19	**Haunting Stories**
19	The Whistler
27	Mysterious Sound
32	Cattle Mutilations
36	Disappearing Tractor
38	The Woman in Black
43	The Old Man Down the Road
47	Grabbed by a Ghost
48	Unidentified Flying Object
49	Roadblock
50	First Encounter
52	Second Encounter
54	Third Encounter
56	Where are the Animals
57	The Black Mass
59	The Grave
76	**Investigations**

76	*June 2010 Investigation*
76	Something's in There
78	Voices from Nowhere
80	The Strangers
81	The Light
83	Confirmation from the Strangers
85	Drumming and Chanting
86	Stan and Belle
90	The Footprint
92	What Opened the Box
94	**The Thrill at the Hill Investigation**
112	Watcher in the Woods
118	The Hunter
122	**My Haunted House on the Hill**
129	Epilogue
133	Campfire Tales Extra
134	Paranormal Witness
134	*The Antique Trunk*
149	About the Author
151	Books by Larry Wilson

DEDICATION

This book is dedicated to all who have experienced the strangeness that the supernatural and the unexplained have to offer. To my colleagues looking for answers to the mysterious and spectacular questions that the paranormal presents to us.

FROM THE AUTHOR

The investigations that led to the writing of this book, were conducted during the daytime and at night. My last nighttime investigation was conducted in 2013. When conducting investigations after hours, I contacted a Shelby County Deputy Sheriff who I originally met at Ridge Cemetery to inform him that I would be in the graveyard after hours conducting paranormal research. In addition, all investigations I conducted whether during daylight hours or during the night, were conducted with the utmost respect to the dearly departed buried in the cemetery as I do at all cemeteries.

Prologue

Humanity has pondered many questions throughout the ages. Questions such as, *"Why are we here on God's green Earth,"* and the age-old question of, *"What is the meaning of life?"*

Many rely on a religious text like the Bible or books by philosophers to seek the answers to the mystery behind our questions.

Of course, the simple answer to, *"the meaning of life,"* is, *"to live and experience our existence."*

In a Christian context, we believe we are here to find and fulfill the purpose God has assigned us.

If we take it a step further and ask, *"Is there life after death?"* Our challenge becomes more complex because it requires navigating the uncharted waters of the unknown.

Books and storytelling are methods used to help us try to understand what lies ahead. They offer theories and legends to explain what may await us once we transition from life as we know it, to life after death.

For me, I must see for myself, because I am too curious to leave it up to stories and legends, preferring to solve the mysteries of the unknown firsthand.

I do this, by exploring places most shy away from, because of the stories and mystery that surround them.

In my travels, I have experienced strange things that defy logic and have caused me to question everything I have been taught about the world we live in.

Williamsburg Hill's Ridge Cemetery and the woods surrounding it are places where many have encountered strange things they cannot explain and have experienced them both during the day and at night.

For decades, bizarre events have occurred at this secluded Illinois graveyard that range from perplexing to terrifying.

Ghostly figures, mutilated cattle, UFO's, and orbs of light with dazzling maneuverability have been witnessed. I have heard disembodied voices and muffled screams coming from beneath the ground.

In this book, you will not only read about the things I witnessed and the evidence I recorded, but will read about eyewitness accounts of others, who also experienced the strangeness that Williamsburg Hill offers.

Accounts like the woman who had a conversation with a man, who after asking her a question, vanished into thin air. Or the mysterious woman in black, who also seems to vanish and who has been witnessed on more than one occasion. You will read about a caretaker's tractor that disappeared without explanation.

Not only will you find these stories convincing and compelling, but downright chilling.

Not all of what I have experienced has been frightening. One event that I have witnessed many times falls more into the category of miraculous.

What I refer to is the gravesite of an adolescent boy where I have witnessed a multitude of women, not knowing anything about the boy or his grave, breakdown and become hysterical with sorrow.

I personally witnessed many of the events detailed in this book, which will serve to give you a firsthand look at the strangeness Williamsburg Hill has to offer. For those of you who are first-time readers of my books, I will give you a brief introduction to who I am, what I do, and why I do it.

My name is Larry Wilson, and I am a former private investigator, turned paranormal investigator and author, who has been looking into the unexplained for over twenty years now.

If you encounter an invisible man sleeping in your bed, and you live in Central Illinois, I am the guy that you would call, not Ghostbusters.

Unlike those who pull the covers up over their head when the paranormal shows up at their doorstep, I seek out the things that go bump in the night, searching for answers to what these ghostly things are and where they come from!

I have investigated the full gamut of the paranormal, from the mundane to the extreme, sometimes with a team of one or two investigators, but most times I investigate alone.

In the twenty years that my journey into the supernatural and the unknown has taken me, I have experienced both the malevolent and the benevolent side of hauntings.

For this reason, I do not treat my investigations as fun and games or a hobby, but with respect and is an endeavor I pursue with purpose and caution.

I write books about my adventures, not to convince people that ghost, and supernatural things are real, but to go on record and document what I have witnessed.

For me, I believe, because I have seen ghostly things with my own eyes and have witnessed many of the fascinating and sometimes terrifying things that the supernatural has to offer.

After reading Strange Williamsburg Hill, I suspect that you

will agree that Ridge Cemetery and the woods that surround it, is a strange and chilling place. But I also suspect you will agree there is something special if not magical about the location, that makes it worthy of visiting again and again.

One advantage of reading and enjoying the adventure into the mysterious world of the unexplained, known as Strange Williamsburg Hill, from the comfort and safety of your favorite chair. Is it gives you time to decide if it is a place you would venture off to alone, after the sun goes down.

THE HILL

The History

As motorist pass through the small Shelby County town of Tower Hill, nothing looks out of the ordinary. What you see is a scene fitting for a Norman Rockwell painting.

The landscape is filled with cornfields, small towns, and modest farms. The world outside their windows looks peaceful and normal.

But if you exit and turn off the main road traveling through the countryside, following one of the many narrow roads in the region, one road will lead you to a whole different world. A world that goes unnoticed as you go about your daily routine.

County Road 1100 East takes you to one of the strangest mystery spots in Central Illinois, Ridge Cemetery at Williamsburg Hill.

Located in the South-Central part of Illinois, not far from the town of Tower Hill, the cemetery is easy to find, as it sits on a ridge at the top of the hill.

The hill itself is unusual, standing over 810 feet high, making it the highest elevation in downstate Illinois.

At one time, a thriving village known as Williamsburg, also called Cold Spring, sat on a ridge near the top of the hill.

Dr. Thomas Williams and William Horsman founded the village in the fall of 1839.

Williams, a medical doctor, had a general store in addition to his medical practice. Upon his death in 1844, his brother Ralph C. Williams took over the practice.

In some journals, the village is described as antiquated and beautifully situated on the ridge.

For some forty years, Cold Spring survived as a thriving village. It housed a blacksmith shop, doctor's office, two churches, a saloon, post office and an eight-room inn used as a stagecoach stop.

The Methodist Church and Masonic Lodge built a large two-story building that served a dual purpose. They used the first floor for church services while the upper floor was used as the Masonic Hall.

Several of the Horsman family members are laid to rest on Williamsburg Hill. Some buried in Ridge Cemetery while others are buried on private property on a farm on the south side of the hill.

The book *"Combined History of Shelby and Moultrie Counties, Illinois"* published by Brink, McDonough & Company of Philadelphia, paints a picture of the wildlife that roamed the land surrounding the village.

Excerpt from the publication

"In the early days, the thickly wooded Hills and clear running streams of this Township attracted deer in large numbers, as well as bear, panthers, wolves, wildcat, turkey and smaller game. Robert Pugh says that when he and his father came here, the elk and buffalo horns could be found quite frequently in this locality, and the sign of the black bear for a number of years afterward could be seen by the practice hunter in the woods, where they would turn over the logs in search of bugs and other insects of which they were fond; strange as it may seem, a bear could turn over a log which would take the combined efforts of two strong men. It was no uncommon thing for the hunter to come upon the carcasses of deer which had been killed and partially eaten by the voracious panther, and with its cat like sagacity, after he had his fill, would cover the remaining carcass with leaves and rubbish; wildcats were numerous, and Mr. Pugh says that he killed 12 one winter. The settlers would frequently suffer much loss from the ravages of wild animals understock of hogs and calves. The early pioneers in this locality seldom shot the wild turkey, as they considered the game too small to waste their precious ammunition on but secured them oftentimes in large numbers in the following manner. They built rail pens with an opening at the bottom and would throw corn on the ground into and around the pen, and when the flock would come, and in feeding on the corn would pass into the enclosure. After the corn was devoured, they would find they were imprisoned, and would endeavor to fly out, not being sagacious enough to escape by the way they entered. Often times whole flocks would be captured in this way." (End)

The reason Cold Spring flourished for so many years, was because of a stagecoach route that ran from Shelbyville to Vandalia and passed through the village. It is rumored that a young lawyer named Abraham Lincoln was at times a passenger of the stagecoach and a guest at the inn. The veracity of this story remains to be seen as I could not confirm this through my search of records. Lincoln did, however, travel from Springfield to Vandalia, quite often.

The stagecoach line brought prosperity to the small community for years, but in 1880, when the Beardstown Shawnee Town and Southeastern Railroad were built, the owners of the railroad bypassed the hill. When this happened, the stagecoach line died out and so did the village of Cold Spring.

Today, little is left of the once thriving village. Only remnants can be found, which are covered by trees and underbrush, a mere memory, invisible to the modern world.

Several families still live nearby, secluded from the hustle and bustle of big city life, but do they live alone?

Just off the main road, hidden amongst the trees and underbrush, is a very odd place, *Ridge Cemetery*.

Although isolated, the graveyard is easily found by looking for a tall microwave tower that can be seen from miles away.

Once you arrive at the tower, turn left, and follow *590 and Counting Road* a quarter mile. As the gravel road narrows, you get the feeling you are driving through a tunnel, due to the close proximity of trees to the road in this highly forested area.

At times, it feels like the trees have eyes, and are watching you. Based on several experiences I had, and stories told to me that you will read about, maybe they do.

You also get the feeling that you are in the middle of

nowhere, and in some respects you are.

What you do not expect, is what awaits you at the end of the road, *Ridge Cemetery*, a place I have found to be shrouded in mystery.

After hearing stories about the graveyard, I expected to find a desecrated place, overgrown by weeds with broken and damaged tombstones.

However, to my surprise, the cemetery is very well maintained.

But well maintained or not, the location is one of the strangest and at times creepiest places I have visited in the years I have been investigating the paranormal.

What separates Ridge Cemetery from other places I have investigated is the mixed bag of paranormal activity that it offers, ranging from ghostly activity to unexplained lights in the sky and graveyard, strange sounds and even objects appearing and disappearing without warning.

I have wandered the cemetery alone, many times, during the daytime and at night. You never know what to expect when you are there.

At times, the cemetery feels peaceful and normal, as one would expect, only to have the environment suddenly change, causing an overwhelming feeling that a presence is watching and following me around the graveyard. It is a feeling that whatever it is, does not want me there.

The feeling has been so overwhelming that I turn around, expecting to see someone behind me, but there is never anyone there. At least no one that I can see.

The graveyard gives you the feeling; you have taken a step back in time, as though you have entered a lost world, alive with some spiritual or otherworldly intelligence.

If you venture down the road at night, you will find a very dark and frightening place as the shadows seem to move and come alive. This, along with the stories of what takes place in the graveyard, is enough to keep most away after the sun sets.

To those who live on the hill, it is home, but for those like me, who pursue the things that go bump in the night, it serves as an invitation to seek out the mystery it has to offer and keeps me coming back, hoping to see more of the strangeness it has to offer.

Haunting Stories

The Whistler

In June 2008, I journeyed alone to Williamsburg Hill for my first nighttime excursion to film a couple of hours of video footage in the graveyard.

It was dark when I arrived, so the first thing I did was unload my equipment and carry it up the hill to the highest point of the cemetery.

Placing my gear near a large oak tree at the center of the cemetery, I began setting up my tripod and video camera to film a variety of shots from different angles for a documentary I was doing.

After filming for thirty minutes, I decided to move the video camera near the gate, at the entrance of the cemetery, and film toward the road.

Having heard stories about a phantom old man seen walking on the road leading to the cemetery who witnesses claim vanishes into thin air. I hoped to be lucky enough to capture the apparition of the old man on video.

I was removing my camera from the tripod preparing to move it, when I heard a loud shrill whistle coming from the woods some forty yards away.

I was facing the entrance of the cemetery to the west, when I heard it, so the whistling was off to my right.

The perplexing thing about it was that it was coming from the woods and I should have heard twigs snapping or movement caused by whoever was in the timber, but I didn't. After all, I was in a rural, secluded graveyard, surrounded by dense woods, and what I would consider treacherous terrain even in the daytime. At night, it is impossible to maneuver through the woods without some type of light. Equally impossible would be maneuvering through the woods without making a sound.

The whistling was unnerving and sent an icy chill down my spine. It did not sound like it was coming from a bird, but from a person. It was the type of whistling someone makes when they take two fingers and place them under their tongue and make a shrill, *"Come here"* type sound.

When I heard it, I stopped dead in my tracks and listened. Everything was still; the birds had quieted and roosted for the night long before I had arrived.

I felt that I was no longer alone and that someone in the forest was watching me.

Trying to talk myself into believing that the whistling must be from a bird, I grabbed my tripod and camera and headed toward the gate.

About halfway between the large oak tree and the cemetery gate, I heard the whistling a second time.

It was the same loud, shrill *"Come here"* beckoning whistle that I heard moments before.

This time, I knew what I heard, and it was not a bird or an animal. The whistling sounded like it was being made by a human, and the sound was unnerving as it echoed throughout the graveyard.

"Someone is whistling for me to come into the woods," I thought to myself.

Even more perplexing, the whistling was closer to me than the first time I heard it, sounding like it was only twenty yards away.

This meant whoever it was, was moving closer to me, or there was more than one of who or whatever was whistling.

Logically, I knew that no one could be in the dense woods at this time of night, without a light or some type of night vision goggles to see.

It was pitch black in the cemetery, so it had to be even darker in the dense forest.

Even with a flashlight it was difficult for me to find my way around the many tombstones in the graveyard, so it would be impossible to navigate through the hazardous terrain of the dark woods without me hearing them. Plus, if they were using a flashlight, I would see them.

Remaining as calm as one can when they are alone in a dark secluded graveyard, I acted like I had not heard the whistling. Because if someone was in the woods, I did not want to give them the advantage of knowing I was aware of them.

Continuing down the hill and through the gate, I set up my tripod in a spot fifteen feet from the gate in the gravel parking lot and another ten feet from the woods to my right, aiming the camera down the road.

As I was placing the camera on the tripod, I heard the whistling again and it sent an icy shiver down my spine. Because somehow, who or whatever it was, was now only ten feet from me at the edge of the timber.

There was no doubt, what I heard. It was the same, beckoning, come here whistle I heard moments before, only it was right next to me.

But how did they get there? It was not possible for anyone to follow me around traipsing through the woods without me hearing them.

I have been in the nearby woods in the daytime and every step you take causes loud crunching and snapping sounds because of the dense underbrush.

From where the first whistling came from, to where it was now coming from, was a distance of seventy-five yards.

I had a straight shot free of obstruction walking from the tree to the parking lot, but somehow whatever was in the woods, beat me to where I was going. This made little sense because of the many obstacles they would have had to maneuver around in order to follow me to where I was going.

Did this strange presence have some pre-cognitive intuition, knowing in advance where I was going to film next?

In complete darkness, even if they had night vision goggles, I should have easily beat the predator to the spot.

Not knowing who or what was lurking in the dark woods was frightening enough, but even more frightening was knowing I was by myself, in a graveyard, located down a secluded dead-end road. If my stalker had sinister intensions, I was on my own!

I tried to remain calm and continued acting as if nothing were wrong. But if I needed to make a fast getaway, I sure wasn't going to leave expensive equipment behind.

Leaving my camera filming, I headed back up the hill toward the tree to retrieve the rest of my equipment. But I didn't head back alone as the whistling followed.

Once again, it moved with me, like it was in pursuit. I had the feeling that whatever was there was daring me to come into the woods.

After making it to my equipment, I opened one of the bags and took out a laser guided digital thermometer to check the temperature in the direction the whistling was coming from. The reason I did this was because many paranormal investigators believe when spirits or supernatural beings are present, there is a drop in the environment's temperature.

I turned on the light to illuminate the screen so I could see the temperature reading in the darkness.

The average temperature was about eighty degrees, but when I pointed the thermometer in the direction, I last heard the whistling, the temperature began to drop.

It slowly dropped from eighty degrees to the lower

seventies, then into the sixties. Suddenly, it hit sixty-six point six degrees Fahrenheit and locked.

Digital thermometers are made to scan the environment for the temperature. I had never seen a thermometer of this type lock on a number.

The temperature stayed on sixty-six point six degrees Fahrenheit for almost thirty seconds.

For those familiar with the Bible, the number 666 has long been linked to the Anti-Christ and is known as the number *of the beast*. The number is also associated with satanism. *"Of all the numbers it could lock on, why this one,"* I thought to myself.

I later found out that the digital thermometer I was using is made for use in the automotive industry, and the range for picking up a temperature is about three feet. So, the temperature I was picking up wasn't coming from the woods but was within a few feet of me.

Whether a coincidence or an omen, the thermometer locking on sixty-six point six degrees, combined with the taunting whistling coming from an unknown source, was the straw that broke the camel's back, so I decided that it was best I pack up and leave.

I gathered up my equipment and headed down the hill to check on my video camera.

As I made the long walk down the hill, the whistling started again like it was following me.

Every twenty feet or so; the shrill whistling would occur. Whatever was in the woods was definitely moving with, taunting, and following me.

The sweat was streaming down my forehead, and my heart

pounding as I walked through the graveyard headed toward the cemetery gate.

"Who is watching me and why are they whistling for me to come into the woods? Is it a ghost or some crazed person up to no good," I thought to myself.

Then it occurred to me that there were unmarked graves of Native Americans buried nearby.

Actually, the graves were just a short distance from the large oak tree and in the direction that the whistling was coming from.

I had read stories about Native Americans communicating by whistling and how they could move about in the forest in a stealth like manner.

If I were dealing with a Native American spirit, or something else supernatural, maybe it could move around in silence without disturbing anything.

When I made it back to my video camera near the gate. I noticed the LCD screen was black, but the camera was still recording.

The only time the LCD screen should go black is if the batteries run down. I had over ninety minutes of battery left, so not seeing the road on the screen using infrared, made little sense.

While checking the camera, I heard the whistling again. It was loud, clear and less than ten feet away, hidden by the underbrush.

"This is getting too close for comfort," I thought to myself.

I felt I had pushed my luck far enough for one night. It was so dark I could barely see my hand in front of my face, let alone a potential ghoul lurking in the woods.

Not knowing who or what I was being pursued by, I selected discretion as the better part of valor and decided to head out and return another day?

I anxiously grabbed my equipment, not bothering to take the camera off of the tripod, folding the legs and laying everything on the front seat of my vehicle.

Placing the key in the ignition, I remember thinking to myself, *"Please start!"*

With the roar of the engine, I felt a sigh of relief and drove off, leaving the dark, frightful graveyard in my rearview mirror, knowing I would be back another day.

As I approached the small town of Pana, I heard a noise on the front seat. Looking to my right, I noticed my video camera was lit up and was filming.

When I left the cemetery, I forgot to power it off and even though it didn't seem to be working when I left the graveyard, it was now.

When I got home, I reviewed the video footage.

I was using an infrared camera, so I should at least have an hours' worth of nighttime footage of the graveyard and road, or so I thought. Because nothing recorded.

Even stranger, my video camera is equipped with audio recording capabilities, and even though the whistling was as close as ten feet from the camera, it was not recorded either, which made little sense.

When I get asked what the most frightening situation I have been in as a paranormal investigator. Without hesitation, my answer is the encounter with the whistling.

Because imagine yourself alone in the darkest, most secluded, graveyard you can think of. Then add to the equation someone or something beckoning you to venture into the woods, using a shrill whistle.

I think you will agree; it doesn't get more frightening than that.

A few months after the whistling incident, I visited a psychic medium friend and told her what happened.

I asked her if she could tell me if what was in the woods had good or bad intentions.

She replied, *"Larry, anything that invites you into the darkness, is never good. Whatever it was, did not have good intentions and meant to cause harm to you."*

I'm not sure what was in the woods that night, but whatever it was, could move about in a stealth like manner and in total darkness.

Since the encounter, I have been to the cemetery many times, and have never heard the whistling again.

Later in the book, you will read about encounters that a logger and a hunter experienced in the nearby woods. I believe it is possible that what they witnessed, may be the allusive whistler.

Mysterious Sound

The Monday morning after my encounter with the strange whistling, all I could do was think about what happened.

I had to tell someone, so I mentioned my experience to two of my coworkers, Cynda and Jim.

Cynda had a casual interest in the paranormal, while Jim, a Vietnam veteran, was a bit more skeptical of ghost and the paranormal. Both however were intrigued by my story.

Cynda believed what I encountered was supernatural while Jim, on the other hand, believe that there was someone in the woods playing tricks on me.

During the discussion, both indicated they would be interested in taking a trip to the cemetery some evening to see the graveyard for themselves.

"How about tonight?" I questioned.

"I'm not doing anything," Jim Replied. *"Neither am I,"* Cynda added.

So, we agreed to meet in the parking lot of the local Walmart in Taylorville at 7:00 P.M., and I would drive the remaining thirty plus miles to Williamsburg Hill.

Jim and Cynda arrived right on time, so we headed out on our adventure.

The sky was overcast when we arrived at the cemetery, with a temperature of 80 degrees.

As we exited the vehicle, I grabbed a camera and my laser pointed thermometer before heading into the graveyard.

We walked up the hill to the large oak tree where I had placed my equipment two nights before and where I first heard the whistling.

I pointed out the area in the woods where the strange whistling originated from.

Both Jim and Cynda agreed the cemetery had a creepy feel to it, although Jim, being the skeptic in the group said it was probably because of being surrounded by the woods.

After giving a brief tour of the graveyard and telling stories about the haunting activity I had read about, we returned to the large oak tree.

As we stood there, I again told the story about what happened Saturday night.

I explained how after hearing the whistling and returning to gather my equipment; I pointed the thermometer in the direction the whistling was coming from to record the temperature.

It was at this point that Jim ask if he could try out the thermometer to see how it worked. Handing the thermometer to Jim, he pointed the device in the same general direction as I did the night of the encounter.

Immediately the temperature dropped. It dropped from eighty degrees to fifty-nine degrees in a matter of seconds.

Fascinated by what was happening, Jim handed the device to Cynda. We were facing north, monitoring the temperature when something happened.

Suddenly, without warning, we heard a loud commotion. My first thought was a speeding car was coming down the narrow road and was going to crash through the cemetery gate.

Simultaneously, we turned toward the timber southwest of the gate.

The noise sounded like a cross between a gale force wind and a locomotive steaming through the woods. The problem is, there was no wind, and no train passes near Ridge Cemetery.

Just as suddenly as it started, the noise stopped and there was dead silence.

"What the hell was that?" Cynda asked in an excited voice. *"I have no idea,"* I replied. It didn't sound like a wild animal or stray cow. It sounded more like turbulent wind, except the night was still and the leaves on the trees were calm, with no movement whatsoever.

I could tell by the look on Jim's face that he didn't have an immediate explanation for what he heard either.

After a brief discussion, we headed to the area where the noise came from to see if there were any downed trees or signs a strong wind had come through. After searching the woods, we found nothing out of the ordinary.

We spent several more hours in the Cemetery but nothing else happened, so we packed up and headed home.

On the drive back, we discussed the incident in depth but still could not come up with an explanation. Jim, half serious and half in jest, wondered if it could have been a large raccoon falling out of a tree.

"Jim, if it were a raccoon," I replied. *"It must have been the size of an elephant."*

Several months after the incident, I ran into a lady who was visiting the cemetery. She told me she frequently visits the graveyard, hoping to witness some of the strange things that she had heard so much about.

I ask her if she had ever encountered anything unusual while visiting the graveyard.

"Well, one afternoon I heard the rumbling of a train and the sound of a train whistle," she replied.

"What I heard was freaky because it didn't sound like a train off in the distance. It sounded like it was passing through the nearby woods."

What the lady heard frightened her enough that she left the graveyard.

Based on the history of Williamsburg Hill and the village of Cold Spring. I wonder if the Beardstown Shawnee Town and Southeastern Railroad, bypassing the hill causing the demise of the village, left such a haunting impression that a phantom train passes through the woods, and at times is heard by visitors to the cemetery.

As crazy as this sounds, I have no other explanation for what Jim, Cynda and I heard or the sound of the train and whistle the lady heard.

It was an uproarious sound and a sound I have never heard

again, while investigating the hill.

Cattle Mutilations

Cattle mutilations, also known as unexplained livestock death, is a mysterious phenomenon that has been going on for years and is believed by many to be associated with UFO activity.

During the 1970s, ranchers and farmers across America were discovering cows and bulls that were not only dead but had been mutilated.

They found the carcasses drained of blood, eyes missing, flesh cut away from the nose and jawbone, the anal cavity cored out, and sex organs removed. The common denominator, with all the incidents, was the blood was completely drained from the carcasses and no sign of animal predation.

Making the mutilations even more mysterious, there were no signs of footprints, or evidence to point to the culprit whether it be human, animal, or paranormal.

To this day, even after thousands of investigations by law enforcement including the FBI, there has never been an arrest for the mutilations.

In the early to mid-1970s, Williamsburg Hill had their own mysterious case of cattle mutilation.

Several books mentioned mutilations taking place on the hill, but no one seemed to know the origin of the stories.

No one, that is, until I stopped at the home of a couple living on the other side of the hill

Both were a wealth of information about the history of

Williamsburg Hill, and as a matter of fact, the wife is the great-granddaughter of William Horstman, who as you will recall, is one of the founding fathers of Cold Spring and along with Dr. Thomas Williams is the eponym of Williamsburg Hill.

I explained I was a paranormal investigator and was doing research for a possible film about the Hill.

Neither wanted to be identified, but both had heard stories and rumors about ghost and odd occurrences in the cemetery but had witnessed nothing themselves.

The husband told me that as a young boy; he camped out in the woods near the cemetery, but his experience was uneventful.

His wife was not a big believer in the supernatural, and she resented the stigma tied to the hill. But, after expressing this to me, she told me a story she remembered her father telling her.

"There is one strange incident I am aware of, that occurred in the 1970s," she said.

With that, she began telling the story her father, who was an eyewitness to the event, told her as a child. When I interviewed the lady, her father was living in a nursing home, so he was not available for a personal interview.

"It happened in the 70s," she began. *"A local farmer found several of his cattle dead in a pasture. It was not apparent how they died, but their reproductive organs, eyes, and tongues were cut out and removed with the precision of a surgeon. They were found on muddy ground and there were no footprints, blood, or signs that an animal was responsible for the deaths of the cattle. All the blood had been drained from their carcasses. If an animal had attacked the cattle, there should have been tracks or traces of blood, but there were none."*

The time period that her father found the mutilated animals fit into the time frame where reports of animal mutilations throughout the United States were numerous.

I asked the husband who raises sheep if he had experienced anything like what his father-in-law had witnessed.

He told me that although he has witnessed nothing like cattle mutilations, several of his lambs have mysteriously turned up missing.

"The puzzling thing about the missing lambs is whatever is taking them, is large enough to jump over the corral fence while carrying them off," he said.

"A coyote is not big enough to hold a lamb in its mouth and jump a fence," he further explained.

Similar to the mysterious cattle deaths, he has never found tracks to identify the culprit.

Several years later I spoke to another resident of the Hill named Leonard, who told me he saw a cougar wandering about in the woods behind his property.

Although large cats are said to be extinct in Central Illinois, there are reports by hunters of finding large tracks resembling those made by Mountain Lions.

With an abundance of deer and small game in Illinois, it is possible that large cats have found their way back to Central Illinois and roam the woods near Williamsburg Hill.

As a result of speaking with a local resident of the hill who you will read about in the section of the book titled, *"My Haunted House on the Hill,"* I was given the name and driving directions to the house of a former Shelby County Deputy Sheriff, who was involved in the 1970s investigation of the mysterious cattle deaths.

Frosty Herron was the Chief Deputy Sheriff at the time and was on the scene of the crime the morning they were discovered.

"It was strange," he said. *"There were several head of cattle, just lying on their sides, dead. They hadn't been shot or stabbed, they ruled out death by electrocution from lightening and there were no signs they were killed by wild animals either. There were no animal or human tracks around the dead cattle."*

"Even stranger, he continued. *There was no blood and all the eyes, rectum and reproductive organs had been removed and they were removed with precision. So, whoever did it, knew what they were doing."*

I asked former Deputy Herron, if he thought it had anything to do with aliens or UFO's, and he said no. He believes that it was done at the hands of someone who knew what they were doing but had no idea why anyone would want to do it. Plus, draining all the blood from several head of cattle would take some time.

He also told me that they couldn't determine the cause of death.

"Cutting the tongue or eyes out of the cattle would cause suffering but should not cause death. When we arrived, it just looked like the cows were laying in the pasture sleeping."

Deputy Herron couldn't recall if it were spring or summer, or the exact year, but said that it was the early to mid-1970s and is sure that it was after 1971.

The mystery of the mutilated cattle was never solved, but as you will also read, during the interview with the local resident in the section titled, *"My Haunted House on the Hill,"* it's possible that a former resident of the hill who is alleged to have been involved in satanic worshiping and ceremonies may have had something to do with it.

Disappearing Tractor

One of the strangest stories I have been told since investigating the paranormal was told to me by a man named Jason.

I met him one afternoon while filming at the cemetery for my documentary.

Jason is one of the caretakers who mows the grass at the cemetery, so he has spent a great deal of time in the graveyard.

One afternoon, he had an experience that he will not soon forget.

Many times, his mother helps him by trimming the grass around the gravestones, while he mows.

On the day in question, they had just finished mowing and trimming the cemetery grass, so he parked his John Deere lawn tractor atop the hill, near the large oak tree at the center of the graveyard. He made sure that the tractor was in gear, so it would not roll.

Jason then joined his mother, and they took a short walk down the hill on the north-side of the cemetery to look at some old gravestones.

After they finished looking at the graves, they returned to the top of the hill. To Jason's surprise, as they neared the oak tree, he noticed the tractor was gone.

From his vantage point, he could see the entire cemetery and the road leading to the graveyard, and the tractor was nowhere in sight.

Jason was dumfounded because he knew it did not simply

roll away, he specifically left it in gear so that would not happen. Besides, if it had rolled or someone had started it up, they would have heard it rolling or heard the sound of the engine, especially since it was a quiet Sunday afternoon.

Even if someone had tried to push it down the hill, they would have heard the commotion.

The tractor was nowhere in sight. It was as though it simply vanished.

Jason and his mother combed the graveyard from one side to the other.

Finally, after an extensive search, they found the tractor in the timber approximately seventy-five yards from where he had parked it, and ten or so yards in the woods.

"We found the tractor turned facing the direction it would have come from, if it had rolled," Jason said. *"It was still in gear, unscratched and unscathed, as though it had been parked there on purpose."*

Now, this is where the story gets even stranger. In order for the tractor to roll, and get from where it was originally parked, to where Jason found it. The following would have had to take place.

First, it would have to pop out of gear, roll down the steep hill, while avoiding several hundred tombstones. Then avoid large trees, downed branches, and shrubs in the dense woods, turn itself around to face the cemetery and place itself back in gear while doing this, causing no damage to the tractor or the trees and brush in the woods.

"It was as though someone or something lifted the tractor and placed it in the timber." Jason said with a puzzled look on his face.

To this day, he still cannot figure out what happened.

Jason told me that some caretakers refuse to work at Williamsburg Hill, due to feelings of being watched and followed. *"They say it's too creepy and they don't like it out here. I can't say that I blame them,"* he added.

He told me the same caretakers work in other cemeteries, but there is something about Ridge Cemetery that frightens them.

The Woman in Black

I heard several chilling stories of encounters with phantoms, while interviewing people who had witnessed them firsthand at Ridge Cemetery.

None, however, were more chilling than the stories of the woman in black. During my investigations and interviews, I talked to two people who witnessed the lady in black.

One witness was a friend and fellow paranormal investigator, Ed Osborne, who had a chance encounter with the woman in black in 2007.

His encounter resulted from the stories I told him about my experiences at Ridge Cemetery, which piqued his interest enough that he took his own road trip to the graveyard with a friend on a Sunday afternoon.

When Ed arrived, he figured they were the only ones there, because no other cars were in the parking area near the entrance to the cemetery.

There is only one way in and one way out of the graveyard, or maybe I should say, there is only one way in and out if you are a living, breathing soul.

To Ed's surprise, when they walked into the cemetery, they noticed they were not alone. Because, in the far southeast corner, there was an elderly woman standing near a graveside.

The odd thing Ed noticed about the woman is she did not look up at them or seem concerned that two strangers had arrived in such a secluded setting. *"You would figure an elderly woman would want to keep an eye on us for safety' sake, especially not knowing what our intensions were,"* Ed told me with a puzzled look on his face.

"We were looking at some older headstones," Ed said. *"I only looked away for a moment, and when I glanced back to where she had been standing, she was gone!"*

"It was like she vanished. Because she would have had to pass by us in order to get to the cemetery gate. Plus, she was dressed in a long black skirt or dress, so she could not have made it through the timber without becoming tangled in the underbrush," Ed explained, shrugging his shoulders.

"The woman appeared to be elderly, so there was no way

she could have maneuvered through the treacherous woods by herself," he added.

Ed was right. The cemetery is surrounded by thick timber and brush and is difficult for a young person to navigate wearing jeans, let alone an elderly woman in a dress.

They searched the area, and the woman was not in the graveyard, nor was she on the gravel road that leads to the cemetery. No other cars were in the parking lot and no other cars came to pick her up. It baffled him where she went.

My interview with the couple who live over the hill took place after Ed told me his story. During the interview, I asked them if they knew of an elderly woman living nearby. They told me they were the oldest couple living on the hill as most of the residents were younger. They did not know of anyone that fit the description of the lady in black.

As Ed was telling me his story, it reminded me of another story one local told me. So, I asked him to describe the old woman to me.

"Well," Ed began. *"She was an older woman, with gray hair that she wore pulled back in a bun. She had on a black dress or skirt that appeared to be from an earlier time period."*

As you will read, Ed's description of the woman in black is significant to another story told to me that took place a year earlier.

The first sighting of the old woman that I heard of was told to me by a lady from Pana named Cathy, who has made regular visits to Ridge Cemetery for years.

She explained that she comes to the cemetery hoping to experience some of the strangeness that the graveyard has to offer, and so far, has not been disappointed. As a matter of fact, you will read about another encounter, that she and her husband Jerry had later in the book.

Cathy's story took place in 2006. On the particular day in question, she was accompanied by her daughter and six-year-old granddaughter.

Their plan was to check out some of the older stones in the graveyard and hang around for a while, hoping to witness something unusual.

Well, as the old Aesop's Fables saying goes, *"Be careful what you wish for, you just might get it."*

When they arrived and entered the cemetery, Cathy and her daughter began looking at old tombstones and her granddaughter wandered off to play in the far southeast corner of the cemetery. As you have noticed, much of the activity seems to take place in the southeast corner of the graveyard.

Her granddaughter had not been gone long when she suddenly came running back, terrified by something.

"When I asked my granddaughter what was wrong, little did I expect what she was going to say," Cathy told me.

"The old woman over there asked me if I wanted to play with the children," the little girl said, pointing toward the corner of the graveyard.

"What woman are you talking about?" Cathy questioned.

To which the little girl replied, *"The woman over there in the black dress."*

Cathy told me she looked in the direction her granddaughter pointed, but no one was there.

Still frightened, her granddaughter continued her story. "When I asked the woman where the children are, she told me, they are under the ground!"

"As soon as she told me this, an icy chill ran down my spine," Cathy said.

"My daughter and I went to the corner of the cemetery to confront the old woman, but when we did, there was no one there and no one else was in the cemetery."

Similar to what Ed told me, Cathy explained that to leave the graveyard, the old woman would have had to pass by them, but she had not, and if she were elderly like her granddaughter said, there is no way she could have made it through the rough terrain of the timber that surrounds the graveyard.

"It was as though she simply vanished," Cathy said.

The location where the little girl encountered the old woman was the same spot Ed Osborne saw her as well.

I asked Cathy if her granddaughter could describe the woman to her.

"Yes," Cathy said. "She was an elderly woman with gray hair, was wearing a black dress, and her hair was pulled back in a bun. My granddaughter said that she looked like an actual person, but when she asked the woman where the children were, and the woman said, under the ground, it scared her, so she came running to us. She was so scared that she didn't bother looking back to see where the woman went."

I believe both Ed and Cathy's granddaughter witnessed the same ghostly woman.

No one seems to know who she is, but the area where she is seen, and Cathy's granddaughter's story of the children playing underground, may apply to an experience I had while investigating in 2010.

It was during the investigation that I heard what sounded like voices coming from the ground. You will read about the incident later in the book.

The Old Man Down the Road

I had heard stories about a vanishing old man in Ridge Cemetery, but little did I expect when I interviewed Cathy from Pana, I would get a two for one interview, as she had a second equally chilling story for me.

In April 2006, Cathy and her husband Jerry traveled to Williamsburg Hill to do some mushroom hunting in the nearby woods.

When they arrived, they backed their pickup truck to the fence next to the gate of the cemetery, then headed into the timber northeast of the graveyard.

Jerry had just made his way down a small embankment when he asked if Cathy would get him a drink out of the cab of the truck before she joined him.

"I made an about face and headed back to the truck to retrieve a drink for Jerry," Cathy said.

"When I made it to the parking area, an elderly man standing in front of our truck startled me."

"I don't know where he came from, because he was not there before, and we didn't pass him on the road on our way in. I guess he could have been in the cemetery, but we should have seen him, and we didn't," Cathy said with a puzzled look on her face.

"One thing I noticed right away; was his appearance and the way he was dressed," she continued.

"He looked odd because he was wearing brown pleated pants, shiny wing-tipped shoes that looked freshly polished, and a silk button-up shirt."

Cathy said his hair was a beautiful grayish silver color and was neatly combed back.

"He was dressed like my grandfather would have dressed, like someone out of the 1920s," she explained.

It puzzled her that the man's shoes were so clean, because it was during the spring, and it had rained earlier that morning.

"He must have walked to the cemetery since there were no vehicles around, so he should have had dirt or traces of mud on his shoes, but they were spotless," she added.

The fact that neither she nor her husband had seen the man on the road perplexed Cathy.

As far as they knew, no one was in the cemetery when they arrived. So where did he come from?

When Cathy approached the truck, she said hello, but he did not reply, which alarmed her even more.

Since the man did not respond to her greeting, she said hello again, and this time he answered, but Cathy could not understand what he said.

When she asked him if she could help him with something, he mumbled his reply, so she said, *"Excuse me?"*

Finally, in a voice she could understand, the man said, *"Can you tell me where the bars are?"*

"When he spoke, I became even more alarmed," Cathy said. "Because I heard him speak and understood what he said, but *his lips and mouth didn't move. It was very creepy."*

Cathy wasn't sure what to tell the old-timer because she didn't know where the closest bar was. They had drinks in their truck, so she offered him one, but the man responded with the same question. *"Can you tell me where the bars are?"*

Just as before, when the man spoke, his lips and mouth didn't move.

Having seen enough, she told the man to wait and she would go ask her husband where the closest bar was. Hurrying down the small embankment, Cathy was met by Jerry, who was curious who this mysterious stranger was.

"What does this guy want?" Jerry asked.

"He wants to know where the bars are," she replied.

Jerry had heard the man from the woods, but had not given

it a second thought, because by hearing the voice, he thought the man was an actual person.

Cathy told her husband he needed to see this guy because something was not right.

With that, the couple made their way up the embankment.

"Jerry started telling him where the bars were, and the man just looked off in the distance and smiled," Cathy said.

"I walked over to my husband, who had a puzzled look on his face. Who is that he asked? Do you know him? To which I replied no."

Cathy and Jerry thought it was odd that a man of his age would be out in the country dressed like he was and no vehicle! When they turned around to look at the man, he was gone!

"Just like that he was gone," Cathy said.

"It was crazy, he was nowhere in sight. There was no way he could have walked away in the short time that it took me and Jerry to turn around."

"We looked everywhere. He was not on the road, because, from our vantage point, the road is visible for a good eighth of a mile. We checked the cemetery, and he was not there. He wasn't dressed to walk through the dense muddy timber surrounding the cemetery, plus we would have heard him moving around in the thick underbrush if he were in there. It was as though he vanished into thin air," Cathy said with a bewildered look on her face.

About a month after the incident, Cathy was talking with a visitor she met at Williamsburg Hill. She said he had maps of the area and seemed to know a little about the history.

She did not mention her encounter with the old man when the stranger started telling a story he heard concerning a traveling salesman who lived in the area many years ago.

As the story goes, the salesman had an argument with his wife, so; he headed out to have a few drinks at a local bar.

Unfortunately, he didn't make it home, because he was killed in an automobile accident on his way back.

Could this be the man Cathy encountered? Is the salesman now a lost soul, searching for the bar where he had his last drink, not realizing it was his final destination. If so, is he now Earth bound for eternity?

Grabbed by a Ghost

I was almost finished writing this book, when I was contacted by a gentleman named Jim Pease, who grew up in Tower Hill, but now lives out of state. He saw a Facebook post of mine about my upcoming book. Jim said he had a couple of stories to share of strange things that he experienced after trips to the hill and Ridge Cemetery. So, I decided to add his stories to the book.

(From Jim Pease.)

"I don't recall the year, but one day my wife and I decided to drive up to the cemetery, so I could visit a friend's grave. My friend's grave is down at the bottom of a hill in the southeast corner of the cemetery and is a good distance from the parking lot, so my wife decided to stay in the car. As I walked to his grave, I kept hearing what sounded like somebody walking through leaves behind me. But when I would turn around to look, no one was there. After my visit was over, I was walking back to the car and was almost to the gate, when I felt a hand grab my left leg. Not only did it startle me, but it also caused me to stumble and I almost fell down. I looked around and didn't see anything, but I know I felt a

hand grab my ankle. My wife was watching me from the car and saw it happen, but she didn't see anything either. To this day, I don't know who or what grabbed me, but someone or something did."

"Another time, my wife and I went for a drive and decided to head over to Williamsburg Hill. It was nighttime and we were halfway up the hill on the north side when inexplicably our headlights started turning off and on. It didn't feel safe to continue, so we turned around and headed home. On the way back, the headlights were fine and didn't turn off once. After we got home my wife's dog Dolly kept staring at the wall for no reason. She kept staring at the wall for hours, like she was looking at something. It was very strange and the timing of her doing this after returning home from the hill made us wonder, if it had anything to do with our trip to the hill."

(Authors note.) I find it interesting that the incident where something grabbed Jim's ankle, occurred shortly after he had visited the southeast corner of the graveyard, where much of the activity seems to take place.

Unidentified Flying Object

During one of my many trips to the hill, I met a local resident who hunts for deer and squirrel in the woods near Ridge Cemetery. He told me about a strange light that he witnessed.

It was the fall of 2008 and he was hunting in the woods near the graveyard.

At one point, he glimpsed something out of the corner of his eye, so he looked up.

Hovering in the sky just above the tree line, he saw a large orange ball of light about the size of a basketball.

"It wasn't an airplane or a helicopter," he said. "It was just a light, and it didn't make any sound. The light hovered for a few seconds then disappeared."

The witness told me that a few minutes after he saw the light, several fighter jets arrived on the scene and circled around the woods above the treetops.

"They acted like they were looking for something, so I figured they were looking for the strange light," he said.

In the summer of 2010, I investigated the cemetery with two paranormal colleagues. One of them saw a large orange light floating above the tree line, then land in the woods just west of the cemetery. What he saw was similar to what the hunter witnessed in 2008.

The 2010 incident will be discussed in the book, in the section titled, *"June 2010 Investigation."*

One unanswered question I have, is whether the cattle mutilations of the 1970s and the strange lights the hunter and my colleague saw, are related.

I asked this question because of the many accounts of cattle mutilations I have read about in newspaper articles, where strange lights were seen in the sky prior to mutilated cattle being discovered.

Roadblock

What you are about to read, boggles the mind, because the events took place right under the nose of the unsuspecting witnesses.

The witnesses telling their stories, do not know each other, but experienced the same phenomena at different times. Their experience was so bizarre you would expect to see it on an episode of the Twilight Zone.

Most have heard the age-old question; *"If a tree falls in a forest and no one is around to hear it, does it make a sound?"*

Well, on the other side of the coin, several of the witnesses I mentioned, were present when a tree fell, but didn't hear it.

First Encounter

I first heard the noiseless tree story, from a family taking a class on the paranormal I was teaching at Lincoln Land College.

For this story, I will use only the first names of the brother and sister, Clayton, and Arianna, who told me the story.

The incident started on Halloween afternoon in 2002 or 2003. It was a nice day, and the weather was calm. Clayton, along with his mother and her friend, arrived at Ridge Cemetery, sometime between one and two o'clock.

They had only walked fifteen or twenty yards into the graveyard, when out of nowhere, they heard a voice.

"It was a female voice and sounded like it came from in front and above us. We all heard it," Clayton explained. *"The voice said, help me!"*

"Even though the weather was calm, a gust of wind blew, and a flock of birds flew over us a split second after we heard the voice. It was weird."

"We stayed a while longer, but nothing else happened, so we left the cemetery. When I got home, I called my sister Arianna to tell her about the voice we heard," he continued.

"Later that day, my sister called and ask if I would like to go back to Ridge Cemetery with her and her boyfriend. I said yes because it was Halloween night. So, the three of us headed to the cemetery in my sister's car."

Clayton described the weather as calm, just like it had been in the afternoon. The only noise the group heard was the crisp sound of rustling leaves as they traipsed about the graveyard.

Since nothing unusual was going on, after thirty minutes, they decided to leave.

"Earlier when we arrived, we made a U-turn in the parking lot so that my sister's car was facing away from the cemetery. When she started the car, the beam from the headlights lit up the road," Clayton explained.

"To our surprise, a log was blocking the lane as if someone or something had deliberately placed it there to keep us from leaving," he further explained.

"My sister stepped out of the car and snapped a photo of the log across the road, because she realized it was not there before and there was no way, it could have fallen or been placed there without us hearing the commotion."

"Getting out of the car, we moved the log to the side of the road, got back in and started to drive off. We didn't get far because another vehicle was heading down the lane toward us. After moving over to let the car pass, we noticed the taillights of the car brighten, and the car stop.

"We wondered if the log was blocking the road again, so we backed up to where the car was," Clayton said.

When they exited the car, sure enough, the log was once again blocking the road.

The sudden appearance and reappearance of the log puzzled them. Plus, if some prankster had dragged the log across the road again, the approaching car should have seen them, but they saw nothing but the log across the road.

The trio believe what they experienced that night was

paranormal, and I agree with them. It would take several people to carry a heavy log and place it across the road, which could be easily done.

What would not be easy is to do so in complete silence and in total darkness, without being seen or heard.

Second Encounter

June 30, 2013, I received the following unsolicited message from a man named Nick. He knew I was a paranormal investigator because his sister-in-law had read one of my first books. He wanted to tell me about a couple of experiences he had at Ridge Cemetery.

(Nick's message)

"When I grew up, I lived just a few miles from Williamsburg Hill, and now live in nearby Pana. I grew up on the same road that leads to the hill, so I have been there many times."

"I never had any experiences until last year, when my wife, sister–in- law and mother-in-law wanted to go there to take pictures of the cemetery."

"One of the strange things I noticed was around a fresh grave. Every photo I took near the grave were partially blurred. After each photo, I checked to see if there was anything unusual in the picture, which is how I noticed the blurring."

"I wiped off the lens to make sure there were no fingerprints or smudges and there were none."

"When I took subsequent photos near other graves, the photos were clear of the blurring."

Author's note. I too have had a similar experience in the graveyard on several occasions. In certain areas, photos were blurry. But when I took photos in other parts of the cemetery, they were clear.

This has happened on more than one occasion at various places in the graveyard.

(Nick's message continued)

"But the strangest thing about the night began shortly after we arrived, when we heard a loud crashing sound that came from the road leading to the cemetery."

"We didn't think much of it at the time, but when we went to leave, there was a full-size tree blocking the road."

"Granted, it's not uncommon for trees to fall, but this tree wasn't dead. It was a healthy tree, full of leaves and was ten inches in diameter."

"The strangest thing about it, it broke off eight or nine feet up the tree, with no apparent reason for it to break."

"It splintered, broke off and fell over. There was no wind, to cause it to snap and fall. It was like something didn't want us to leave."

"We were in my wife's car, so I couldn't drive over it, and it was too heavy for us to move, so I called my father-in-law to bring his chainsaw to cut it up and move it off the road."

"My father-in-law is a skeptic when it comes to the paranormal, but even he thought it was odd the way the tree broke off and fell."

"If what happened wasn't creepy enough, while we were waiting for him to arrive, we heard loud banging and knocking sounds and we couldn't figure out what was *causing them."*

Authors note: The only difference in what Nick and his family experienced in comparison to what Clayton and his sister encountered, was they heard the sound of the tree falling, while Clayton and Arianna did not. But what caused a healthy tree to snap and fall?

(July 6, 2013 message from Nick)

"We went up to Ridge Cemetery again last night to take a few photos. The environment felt different in the cemetery. It was a heavy feeling. I smoke, so I had a cigarette in the parking lot when we first arrived and didn't notice anything unusual. Later, while walking around the graveyard, I had another one and the smoke literally lingered in the thick air."

"We kept hearing unusual sounds in the timber. It sounded like someone was stomping their feet. I'll be honest with you, I try to be skeptical, and explain things that happen using logic, but for some reason things just seem weird in Ridge Cemetery."

Third Encounter

In November 2015, I held a book release party for my third book, Dark Creepy Places at Krieger's restaurant in Taylorville, Illinois.

While I was setting up for the event, a waitress approached me and asked what my book was about. When I told her I investigate the paranormal, she asked if I had ever heard about Williamsburg Hill.

"Yes," I said. "I have investigated there many times."

"Boy, do I have a weird story for you that happened to me one night," she said. "Please tell me, I would love to hear the story," I replied.

"It happened a couple of years ago when several of my friends and I drove over to Ridge Cemetery to see if we could experience anything unusual. When we arrived it was dark, so we made a U-turn and parked the car, so it was facing away from the cemetery," she explained.

"We had only been there for an hour, but since we had seen nothing, we decided to leave. When we started the car, and the headlights came on, to our surprise, there was a large log laying across the road, blocking our exit. What was creepy about it, was we didn't hear a tree fall or anyone dragging the heavy log across the road, and you hear every sound when you are out there. It was crazy."

Knowing Clayton and Nick's stories, I asked her if she knew either of them, and she did not.

So, three groups of people, not knowing each other, told me similar stories that occurred at different times.

To me, the strangest thing about the trees across the road is the fact that neither Clayton's group nor the waitress heard anything, and the road was clear when they arrived.

I have been in Ridge Cemetery on many nights and can attest that no matter how insignificant the sound is in the nearby woods, you hear it.

Even though Nick and his family heard something falling, they couldn't explain what caused a healthy tree to snap and fall over.

Especially when there was no wind to cause it to break.

So, does someone or something in the woods watch people visiting the graveyard and try to prevent them from leaving?

If so, then what can cause a tree to fall or drag a log across a road, without making a sound?

The answer my friends; is nothing in the physical world can!

Where are the Animals?

There are so many strange occurrences taking place at Ridge Cemetery and in the nearby woods, that it is hard to pinpoint which phenomena is the strangest.

One unusual thing that stands out to me in my over one-hundred investigations at Ridge Cemetery, is the lack of animals in and around the graveyard.

I am not saying they are not there, but I have seen very few in the fourteen years I have been going to the cemetery.

I have found a few deer tracks in the timber but have never seen a deer in the woods or graveyard. The subdivision where I live near Taylorville is located close to a small timber and I see deer all the time. But this is not the case in the woods surrounding Ridge Cemetery.

Equally unusual are the lack of squirrels and small animals. There is an abundance of oak trees in the graveyard loaded with acorns, but I have never seen a squirrel or rabbit in the cemetery. I know they are in the nearby woods because I have talked to outdoorsman who hunt them.

Likewise, with the many trees in the cemetery, one would think they would be loaded with birds, but they are not. Don't get me wrong, I see birds in the area, but for some reason they avoid the graveyard.

At night, the burial ground is abundant with mammals in the form of bats devouring the many flying insects, but during the day, the bird population is sparse for no apparent reason.

Two of the witnesses I mentioned, Cathy and Nick both brought up the lack of birds and animals in the cemetery, without prompting from me. So, it is not my imagination; they noticed this too. Later in the book you will read about an interview I did with a hunter, and he too has noticed the lack of small animals on Williamsburg Hill.

Of the many cemeteries I have been to, Ridge Cemetery, is the only location where small animals seem to shy away from.

Some theorize that the nearby microwave tower gives off a frequency that affects the animals. If this were true, you would think the microwave tower near the timber by my house would affect the animals, but it doesn't.

For now, the lack of animals and scarcity of birds in the graveyard is just another oddity that makes Ridge Cemetery so strange.

The Black Mass

I have heard stories of black panthers roaming Williamsburg Hill but have never found tracks or evidence of them myself.

With that being said, two witnesses I talked to may have seen the creatures for themselves.

One story was told to me in 2007, by a man named Jerry. Although he is not sure what he saw, what he described sounds like the mannerisms of a big cat.

The following is Jerry's story.

"One night a few years ago, a friend and I drove to Ridge Cemetery to hang out. We wanted to see if we could experience any of the strange things people claim to see out there. It was around dusk, so it was getting dark. I admit we drank a couple of beers, but we were not intoxicated. My truck was backed up to the fence, and we were sitting on the tailgate talking. We had been there about forty-five minutes, when we heard something big rustling in the large oak tree

in the center of the graveyard," Jerry explained.

The tree Jerry is referring to is the same tree I placed my camera equipment under the night I encountered the strange whistling. So, from the parking lot, they were at least forty yards from the tree.

"Whatever it was, was big and we could hear it moving around in the tree," Jerry continued.

"Then suddenly, a large black shadow leaped from the tree and landed a good twenty-five yards from the tree. Then it leaped again and landed in the timber, which was another twenty-five yards from where it had first landed. After this thing entered the woods, there was dead silence. There was no movement or sound like you would expect from something as large as this thing was. My first thought was it had to be a black panther jumping out of the tree. Because I had heard stories of big cats and panthers seen on the hill. Plus, what else could it have been?"

Although Panthers have powerful hind legs allowing them to jump 15 to 18 feet off the ground and into trees. They cannot leap twenty-five yards like Jerry witnessed.

I asked Jerry if they saw or heard anything else that night, and his reply was, *"Heck no, that was all we needed to see, we got out of there."*

In 2010, a paranormal colleague and I talked to a resident named Leonard, who at the time lived near Ridge Cemetery in a small camper.

He told us about the time a few years earlier when he heard something big moving through the timber behind his home.

When he investigated, he saw a mountain lion walking through the woods.

Leonard had been burning a large pile of old papers and when he lit it, the fire quickly crackled to life. When it did, he heard the roar of a big cat. *"I think the crackling from the burn pile startled the cat,"* he said.

Leonard said there is a forty-foot drop off behind his camper, and at the bottom of the drop-off is an old, wrecked station wagon he believes the cat was using as its den.

I have often wondered if large cats roaming Williamsburg Hill, could explain the lack of small animals in the cemetery and the missing lambs that the witness told me about. But what type of feline can leap twenty-five yards like Jerry described?

The Grave

Sometimes, mysteries are discovered by accident rather than good detective work, which is the case with the next story.

I must add that normally, I do not give specific details about graves, in order to protect individual privacy. But because of spectacular events that took place at one grave, I must give certain details that corelate to events that took place.

From 2006 to 2010, I investigated Williamsburg Hill alone, then in 2010, I began bringing others with me to investigate. It wasn't until July 2010, that the first female investigators came with me to the cemetery.

It was at this time; I made a discovery that offered discernible evidence of an invisible world, that not only interacts and intersects with us, but affects our emotions and perceptions as well.

This unexpected interaction, offers hope, and strengthens my faith, that there is life after death. In addition, little did I realize I would witness this strangeness many times in the future.

On the first night in question, two paranormal colleagues accompanied me. Chris, a male investigator, and a female investigator named Janet.

We arrived at the Cemetery at 9:00 P.M. The sky was overcast, so the graveyard was darker than usual. It was so dark; I could not see my hand in front of my face without using a flashlight.

This was Janet's first trip to Ridge Cemetery, so I gave her a brief tour and told her about some of the unusual activity I had experienced.

After unloading our equipment, we headed toward the far southeast corner of the graveyard and were passing through the area where Ed Osborne and Cathy's granddaughter saw the woman in black.

I recently met Janet, so I didn't know her very well. One of her claims was that she is sensitive to spirits. Not being around her enough to know if she was clairvoyant or not, I had not formed an opinion to the validity of her claim.

As we continued our trek toward the southeast corner, Janet suddenly stopped and declared that an old woman in a navy-blue dress was standing nearby.

Neither Chris nor I saw anything, but Janet was adamant that she was looking at an old woman who was standing near a gravesite.

Realizing we were in the vicinity where the old woman was seen; I asked Janet to describe what she was seeing.

"She is an older woman, wearing an outdated, navy-blue, full-length dress. Her hair is pulled back in a bun. She is

telling us to be careful," Janet said.

"Wow," I thought to myself. *"Janet doesn't know the story about the woman in black, and she just perfectly describe what Ed and Cathy's granddaughter saw."*

The only difference in her description was the color of the dress, which Janet said was navy-blue.

"It would be easy to mistake navy-blue for black during the daytime, maybe there is something to Janet's clairvoyance," I thought to myself.

After she described the old woman, I told Janet and Chris about Ed and Cathy's encounter with the woman in black, then we continued to our destination.

We were standing in front of a grave near the corner of the cemetery when Janet started crying.

"What's wrong, Janet?" I asked.

"I don't know, I just feel sad all of a sudden."

"What are you sad about?"

"I'm not sure, but I get the feeling it has something to do with this grave," she said, aiming the beam of her flashlight at the grave.

Her light lit up the uniquely shaped headstone of a young boy. Upon researching the boy's name, I found that he was a passenger in a car involved in an accident and was killed.

I put my hand on Janet's' shoulder to comfort her, but my gesture didn't help, as she was now sobbing more than ever.

No matter what we said or did, Janet could not stop crying, so we moved away from the grave, and her emotions returned to normal.

Later that night, we returned to the grave and once again, Janet became emotional. But why?

I thought it strange that the grave only affected Janet and not Chris or me. But, if Janet were sensitive to spirits like she claimed, she may have picked up on emotions that neither of us would. So, I didn't give it much thought.

Several weeks later, I found out, that the strange reaction Janet experienced near the grave, was not exclusive to her.

It was a Saturday night. I brought paranormal colleagues,

Carl Jones, John Jenner, and a woman named Laura with me to the cemetery. They had heard me tell stories about the graveyard and asked if I would take them out there to see it.

We arrived at the Cemetery at sunset, so; it was not quite

dark yet, but the shadows had set in. We were near the large oak tree having a conversation, when I noticed that Laura was missing.

Surveying the cemetery with my eyes, I spotted her standing in the southeast corner near the boy's grave. Thinking it was odd that she had wandered off in the darkness alone, I headed toward her to see what she was doing.

When I got within a few yards of her, in order not to startle her, I called out. *"Laura, are you OK?"* But there was no response.

When I got to where she was standing, I noticed that she seemed upset and was sobbing.

"What's the matter?" I asked.

"I don't know," she replied. *"It's really weird. Something about this corner caught my interest, so I came over here. But I'm not sure why. Then suddenly I felt overwhelmed with sadness."*

As I was talking to Laura, I noticed she was standing next to the grave of the boy where Janet had also, unexpectantly, become emotional.

"Wow, this is too strange to be coincidence," I thought to myself. Plus, why would Laura wander off in the dark shadows alone, when she knew that as a group, we were headed to this corner of the graveyard next? Was it coincidence or did something supernatural coax her to the corner?

In the words of famed mystery writer Agatha Christie's detective Ms. Marple. *"Any coincidence is worth noticing. You can throw it away later if it is only a coincidence."*

The common denominator of Janet and Laura's emotional

reactions was they occurred next to the young boy's grave.

A short time later, Carl and John joined us, and we discussed what happened. Like before, no one else reacted emotionally.

Since we were not investigating, after I finished showing the group around the graveyard, we left.

When I got home, I pondered what happened to Janet and Laura.

The only commonality to the emotional outburst were the boy's grave and the parties who reacted were female. But why?

Later in the book, you will read about an investigation that I conducted at Ridge Cemetery, with a local radio station, 99.7 KISS FM. I call the investigation, *"The Thrill at the Hill Investigation,"* which took place in September 2012.

I bring up the investigation now, in order to discuss how a female intern who was part of the investigation, and who knew nothing about the boy's grave or how females react when near it, had her own emotional experience at the grave.

I will discuss the complete investigation in full, in the section titled, *"The Thrill at the Hill Investigation."*

The intern, Taylor Fishburn, is known on air by her nickname, *"Tunamelt."*

Also accompanying me on the investigation, was Taylor's boss, morning show radio personality, Jason "Bondsy" Bond and his co-host Sarah.

Before heading out for the investigation, I told Bondsy that I would like to try an experiment with the girls when we arrived at the Cemetery. I told him how I had witnessed females who approached a particular boy's grave, become emotional. Then told him the name of the boy.

The experiment would be nothing more than having the girls stand by the grave one at a time, then ask them to tell me how they felt.

Since this was the first time the radio crew had been on a paranormal investigation, they were a bit on edge, primarily because they didn't know what to expect.

Adding to their apprehension were the stories I told, of things I had experienced at the graveyard during my investigations, including running into shady characters in the parking lot at night, who were doing drugs.

We set up our base camp for the night, ten yards from the boy's gravesite. After doing a walkthrough of the graveyard, I placed audio recorders and a video camera in strategic locations in the cemetery. Then it was time for my experiment.

There are several graves near the boys, so I guided Sarah in the obscure darkness to the grave and told her to stand still. Because of the darkness, she could not see any identifying information on the gravestone.

Once Sarah was in position in front of the grave, I backed away, then ask her to tell what she was feeling.

"Nothing in particular," she said.

"You don't feel anything," I questioned. *"No, not really,"* she replied.

After standing by the grave for a couple of minutes without reacting, I thanked Sarah, and asked her to move away from the grave. I then guided Taylor to the spot where Sarah had been standing. *"Ok Taylor, tell me how you feel,"* I said. Immediately, she replied. *"I don't know what is going on, but I am starting to get emotional."*

"Do you feel anything else," I asked, trying to steer her focus away from the feeling of sadness.

"No, I just feel really sad."

"No way," Bondsy exclaimed. "You told her about what happens, didn't you?"

"I didn't tell anyone about what happens except for you, Bondsy," I replied.

"I'm not sure what you are talking about," Taylor interjected. "But Larry didn't tell me anything."

"Wow, then that's crazy!" Bondsy added.

So, one of the two girls became emotional, but why didn't Sarah?

A few days later, Bondsy and I had a conversation about the graveside experiment.

I told him I couldn't figure out why Sarah didn't become emotional at the grave like other females did.

"*Larry, Sarah was so scared of the possibility of critters in the woods and the drug dealers you mentioned showing up, that she wouldn't have felt anything if a ghost was standing next to her,*" Bondsy said.

Bondsy's analogy that fear prevented Sarah from becoming emotional was definitely a possibility.

But as you continue reading, you will hear a different take from a female test subject, I took to the graveyard who also became emotional at the boy's grave.

It was in the late summer of 2015, when I invited a friend named Shelly to the graveyard. The only thing I told her was I wanted to conduct an experiment related to my paranormal research. I didn't mention the grave or anything about the boy buried there.

We arrived at the Cemetery at 7:00 PM. It was still daylight, so I gave Shelly a quick tour of the graveyard and told a few stories of things I had experienced, and stories others had told me.

At 8:00 o'clock we headed toward the boy's grave. Shelly was not aware what the experiment was, so she had no idea what to expect.

When we got close to the grave, I had her turn, so that her back was to the grave and she could not see the boy's gravestone.

I guided her backwards until she was in front of the grave. Then I said, *"Close your eyes and tell me what you feel."*

After a few moments, she started getting teary-eyed and said, *"I feel really sad."*

"Why do you feel sad," I asked.

"I am not sure. But I think it has something to do with the grave behind me. It is not the feeling of sadness because of death, it's a mother's sadness, like mourning a lost child that I miss very much."

With that, I turned Shelly so she could see the grave and the boy's headstone. I noticed her take her index finger and wipe away a tear running down her cheek.

There is a nearby grave only a few feet to the left of where the boy is buried.

The person buried there is a woman, much older than the boy who has the same last name. She passed away a short time after the boy was killed. I have always wondered if the woman is the boy's grandmother.

Shelly didn't notice the grave, so I asked her to turn around again, so that her back was to it.

I guided her to my left, so that she was standing in front of the woman's grave, with her back to it.

"Shelly," I said. *"Tell me how you feel now?"*

"I still feel sad, only now the feeling is the sadness a grandmother would feel toward her grandson and for her daughter or son who lost a child."

"No kidding?" I questioned in a surprised tone of voice. *"Turn around and look at the grave behind you,"* I added.

When she turned toward the grave, I explained to Shelly my speculation that the woman could be the boy's grandmother. *"And now you tell me you are feeling a grandmother's sadness,"* I said. *"What is the chance of that?"*

This would not be the last time I would witness the strangeness that takes place near the young boys' grave.

In October 2016, I took friends, Nicole Richards-Featherstone, her sister Kylee Kahbeah, and Todd Kahbeah, who is stepfather to Nicole and father to Kylee, to Ridge Cemetery for an investigation.

Nicole, a friend, and co-worker at the Illinois State Board of Education where I worked, asked me if I would take the trio on an investigation somewhere.

Although Nicole is anxious when it comes to ghost and things that go bump in the night, I knew Kylee and Todd had a strong interest in the paranormal since the three had accompanied me on an investigation a couple of years prior.

"Sure," I responded to Nicole's question. *"But on one condition." "What is that?"* She questioned with a laugh.

"I would like to conduct an experiment with you and Kylee. It is nothing scary nor anything you will be left alone to do. If what I think will happen, happens. It will amaze you."

Even though neither Nicole nor Kylee knew what to expect, they agreed to take part in the experiment.

In late October, I met the trio in the parking lot of the local Taylorville Walmart, and we headed to our destination in my SUV.

When I turned off the main road and headed down road 1100 East, the girls started getting a bit nervous.

With the close proximity of the timber on either side of the narrow road, it gets pitch black in a hurry, and can be a frightening place.

It's not somewhere you want to get stranded in the middle of the night.

The road offers the type of setting you would expect to find in a horror movie. As your headlights light up the narrow lane, you half expect to see a ghoulish figure standing in the road waiting for you.

It was 10:00 P.M. when we arrived at the cemetery. I made a U-turn in the gravel cul-de-sac before I parked to make for an easy exit when we were ready to head out.

As I was unloading my equipment, Nicole noticed a metal baseball bat in the hatchback compartment of my vehicle.

I explained to her that since I don't own a gun; I bring it with me to secluded locations for protection. Several times while alone at Ridge Cemetery, I have stumbled upon what appeared to be drug transactions taking place. So, I bring the bat just in case.

On this night, the baseball bat would be important for another reason. You will understand the significance of the bat, momentarily.

Our base camp for the night would once again be at the far southeast corner of the graveyard, near the boy's grave.

Since everyone had to work the next day and Kylee had school, the plan was to investigate until 2:00 A.M. To save time setting up and breaking down equipment, I only brought a video camera, several audio recorders, and a digital camera.

We also brought camping style chairs, which we sat up in the corner near the timber.

After establishing our base camp, and setting up the equipment, we did a walkthrough of the graveyard. I told a few stories of things I had witnessed to set the mood.

Our walkthrough ended back at base camp. Since it was close to the boy's grave, I decided it was time to conduct my experiment with the girls.

I led the group to a spot no more than eight feet in front of the grave. It was so dark in the cemetery, the girls could not see the headstone, let alone see that a young boy was buried in the grave.

Todd and Kylee waited as I guided Nicole to a spot a few feet in front of the grave. I positioned her so she was facing away from the boy's final resting place.

"OK," I said. "Nicole, all I want you to do is tell me how you feel."

"How I feel?" She questioned.

"Yes," I said. *"Just tell me how you feel."*

"Oh wow! All of a sudden, I feel sad and am getting emotional."

"No kidding," I replied. *"You don't feel anything else?"* I questioned, trying to steer her away from the emotion of sadness.

"No, I just feel very sad and am all teary-eyed," she replied.

With that, I took Nicole by the hand and guided her to where Todd and Kylee were standing.

"That was really weird," Nicole interjected.

"Yes, it was." You don't know why you were feeling emotional, I questioned.

"No, it was just weird!"

"OK, Kylee, your turn." I said, as I took her hand and guided her to the front of the grave where Nicole had stood.

"OK, same thing Kylee, just tell me how you feel!"

Barely getting the word feel out of my mouth, Kylee started sobbing uncontrollably.

I had witnessed various women crying at the boy's grave, but nothing like this. Kylee was having an emotional breakdown. *"Are you all right Kylee,"* I questioned as I grabbed onto her as it appeared, she was going to drop to her knees.

"I'm not sure what happened. Something came over me,"

she said, still sobbing.

With that, I guided her away from the grave to where Todd and Nicole were standing.

After making sure that Kylee was all right, I told the group what the experiment was and how their reactions were exactly what I had expected.

I contacted Nicole, Kylee, and Todd during the writing of this book to get their take on what they experienced at Ridge Cemetery that night.

Collectively, they were astonished by the girl's reactions at the gravesite. But more so were bewildered by Kylee's extreme reaction. Nicole told me that of the two, she is the emotional one, not Kylee.

"I had a sense of sadness and became teary-eyed, but my reaction was nothing like Kylee's. I couldn't believe it. Nicole said.

"I didn't understand what was happening," Kylee added. *"I am not the type of personality who becomes emotional or cries. But I couldn't control what was happening. It was really strange."*

The rest of the night was uneventful, or so it seemed. Because two days later, when I was reviewing data from the audio recorder, I had placed next to the boy's grave, I found an unaccounted-for voice, or what is known in the paranormal field as an EVP.

EVP stands for *"Electronic Voice Phenomena,"* which are voices and sounds that are recorded by audio and video recording equipment, the source of which is unknown. Sometimes the voice or sound is heard at the time it is recorded, but many times it is not, which was the case in this instance.

The voice sounds like an adolescent child and was recorded at 1:50 A.M., as we were walking toward the grave to gather up our equipment and head home.

In the recording, as we near the grave, you hear Kylee ask, *"What time is it, I forgot to look?"* This is followed by Todd responding and saying, *"1:30,"* immediately followed by Nicole saying, *"1:50."*

As soon as Nicole says, *"1:50,"* the adolescent sounding voice asks, *"Can I swing it?"*

When I found the voice, I sent a text message to Nicole asking for her email address, then emailed an audio clip of the voice.

Nicole shared the EVP with her sister and Todd, and they all heard exactly what I heard.

Nicole sent me a follow-up text which said.

"Larry, do you think since the boy is dressed like a baseball player in a photo on his headstone, that he is referring to the baseball bat in the back of your car we were talking about when we arrived, and is asking if he can swing it?"

I hadn't thought about that, but what Nicole said made sense, and I now believe that the voice could be that of the boy and agree with Nicole's analogy that he is asking if he can swing the bat.

In November 2014, the Christian County Genealogical Society in Taylorville, Illinois, asked me to speak about my work as a paranormal investigator.

Sixty-eight people attended, so it was a good-sized crowd. The announcement of the event in the local newspaper listed several of the places I had investigated, including Ridge Cemetery at Williamsburg Hill.

During my lecture, one thing I talked about was the emotional reaction that women have at the boy's gravesite.

I try to be respectful by not giving the boy's name out to minimize the chance of people disturbing his grave.

At the end of my presentation to the group, I asked if there were any questions and there were none.

As I was packing my materials, a woman stopped by the table I was sitting at.

"Mr. Wilson, may I ask you a question," she inquired.

"Yes, you may," I responded.

With that, she took out her cell phone and began looking through her photos.

"I want to show you a picture," she said. "Sure," I replied.

"Is this the boy's grave that you are talking about?" She questioned.

When she showed me the photo, I was surprised, because indeed, it was a photo of the boy's grave.

"Yes, it is," I answered. "How did you know?"

"Well," she began. "Last week, I drove over to Ridge Cemetery at Williamsburg Hill, to walk around the graveyard. Everything was fine until I stopped at the grave of the young boy. When I did, just like you said in your presentation, I became emotional and started sobbing. I was crying uncontrollably and couldn't stop. I was crying so hard; I had to leave the cemetery. When I got to my car, I could finally stop crying."

"Were you aware of the boy or his grave before you went

to the cemetery?" I asked.

"No, I knew nothing about him," she replied. *"Then I saw in the newspaper that you were giving a presentation on the paranormal and one of the places you were going to talk about was Ridge Cemetery. I thought I would come and ask you if you knew anything about the boy or his grave and tell you what happened to me. Little did I expect that you would discuss exactly what I experienced."*

The woman's experience was further proof that something strange takes place at the boys' grave. But why his grave and not others?

Based on what I have witnessed and the experiments I have conducted. Only females become emotional at the grave. In addition, the reaction must be spontaneous.

I say this, because when I tested other women and told them what takes place at the boy's grave beforehand, they did not react.

A good example of this was a night I took a local sorority group to the cemetery.

There were five women in the group, all of which knew beforehand I had witnessed women sobbing at the grave.

Just as I had done previously, I had each of the group, one by one, stand by the grave, but none reacted. One would think that knowing a young boy is buried in the grave would cause an emotional reaction more so than not knowing who is buried there, but it doesn't.

So, for whatever reason, there is something about the boys grave, that affects the emotions of unsuspecting women without foreknowledge of the boy or what happens at the grave. Why they react at his grave and not others, is a true paranormal mystery.

Investigations

Since 2006, I have investigated Ridge Cemetery many times. But two investigations stand out compared to the others, because those who were with me also got to see the strangeness that the graveyard has to offer, firsthand.

The investigations took place, July 10, 2010, and September 28, 2012, when I took the local radio station's morning show crew I mentioned earlier in the book.

July 10, 2010 Investigation

Accompanying me on the expedition were investigators Chris and Janet. Janet was new to paranormal investigating, but as you will recall from earlier in the book, seems to be sensitive to spirits. So, she had been in touch with the spirit side of the paranormal for some time.

During the July investigation, we experienced several strange things that we could not explain, and as it turned out, would be one of the most active nights of any of my investigations at Ridge Cemetery.

Something's in There

Shortly after arriving, we headed to the corner of the graveyard, near the boy's grave, and set up our base camp.

We wouldn't have to wait long, because it would be only a matter of minutes before the strange activity started.

Chris sat on a wooden bench next to the fence by the timber. Janet and I had folding chairs that we sat up ten feet or so from Chris.

At night, the Cemetery is very dark, and the surrounding timber is even darker, making the perfect setting for a paranormal investigation.

We were sitting and listening to the sounds of the woods when Chris stood up and said, *"It feels like there's someone standing behind me! The hair is standing straight up on my neck!"*

With that, Chris turned around looking behind him and asked me to shine my flashlight to see if anything was there.

I aimed my light in the direction he indicated, but we saw nothing.

A few minutes later, we heard something big moving around in the woods. It was less than fifteen yards from us.

I shined my flashlight in the direction of the movement, but nothing was there. We could see the tall underbrush moving about like something large was hiding. Then the movement stopped.

Picking up a walnut that was lying nearby, I threw it into the woods, hoping to stir whatever it was.

Within seconds, the walnut came flying out of the woods, landing next to Chris, and bouncing against his leg. We knew that the walnut didn't fall from a tree, because we heard the sound of the object as it deflected off leaves as it made its way through the woods and landed against Chris's leg. Something had thrown the walnut.

"What the hell," Chris said, as we looked at each other in disbelief. We threw a couple more walnuts in the direction where the movement had been, but nothing happened.

Searching the woods with my flashlight, I saw nothing. So, I took several photos of the area behind the bench and reviewed them using the LCD screen of my camera.

In one photo, there was a strange, vibrant red mist.

I'm confident it was not dust, pollen, or moisture, because part of the mist was behind a tree branch, which meant the branch was between my camera lens and the mist.

So, whatever it was, was not something on or near the lens of my camera.

I have taken pictures with mist in them before, but never mist that was bright red. There was nothing red in the timber or around us that would have caused a red reflection. To this day, I cannot determine what it is.

While looking at the photo of the red mist on my camera, I heard what sounded like a muffled scream.

Voices from Nowhere

"Do you guys hear that?" I asked.

"Hear what?" Questioned Chris.

"It sounds like someone is screaming, but it is faint," I answered.

"I hear it too," Janet added.

As we stood there listening, it happened again.

"Now I hear it," Chris said. *"It sounds like its off in the distance."*

Moments later, we heard it again, only this time it sounded like multiple people were screaming. *"Is it coming from the woods?"* I questioned.

"I don't know," Chris responded. *"But it is definitely screaming."*

As the wailing continued, I noticed it didn't sound like it was coming from a distance but sounded like it was coming from beneath us.

"*Guy's, listen close,*" I said excitedly. "*The screams aren't coming from the distance; they are coming from the ground!*"

"*What, coming from the ground?*" Chris said in a questioning tone.

"*You're right, Larry!*" Janet added. "*They are coming from the ground!*"

As we continued listening to the screaming, we determined they were coming from directly beneath us.

Then I remembered what eyewitness Cathy told me about her granddaughters' conversation with the old woman.

If you recall, the granddaughter said that when the old woman approached her and asked her if she wanted to play with the children. The girl asked where the children were. To which the woman replied, *"They are under the ground!"*

So, were we hearing the screams of the children the old woman referred to? The area the screams were coming from was the same area where Cathy's granddaughter had her encounter.

It sounded like people were trapped in an underground cavern, but how?

Was there some type of doorway to the other side beneath us?

The screaming continued for several minutes, then suddenly stopped.

Although we would not hear the screams again, it would not be the last time they would be heard on this night.

The Strangers

As we were discussing the voices, we heard a car coming down the lane to the graveyard.

"Hey, somebody's coming," Chris announced.

I turned to look and saw headlights coming down the narrow lane.

"It's probably the Shelby County Sheriff's office," I said. *"I met the deputy that patrols out here and he told me he was okay with me investigating in the cemetery. He comes out here looking for kids drinking and vandalizing the graveyard."*

Thinking it was the sheriff's office, we headed toward the parking lot to let them know who we were and what we were doing.

To our surprise, it was a woman and her teenage nephew from Mattoon, Illinois.

They told us they had heard about Ridge Cemetery and its reputation of being haunted, so they drove over hoping to experience some of the strangeness it was noted for.

The woman, who I estimated to be in her forties, was drinking and appeared to be on the verge of intoxication.

The boy, in his early teens, was nice and seemed to have a genuine interest in the paranormal. When he found out we were paranormal investigators, he became excited.

"Have you guys seen anything weird tonight?" He asked.

Even though we had already experienced several strange things, I told the boy that everything was quiet.

I told him this, because we had audio and video equipment set up, and I was afraid that their voices would interfere with our recordings. Especially with the vociferous voice of his nearly intoxicated aunt rambling on. So, by telling them nothing was going on, I hoped they would leave.

Unfortunately, my ploy failed, and they decided to stick around for a while.

Since the strangers were hanging around, I suggested that we take a walk down the lane leading to the cemetery and see if we could record anything. Then by the time we came back, hopefully the strangers would be ready to leave.

Not trusting our uninvited guest, we returned to our base camp and grabbed our chairs. We thought it best to lock them in our vehicle in case the duo decided to run off with them.

The Light

As we headed toward the vehicle, we decided to sit for a few minutes under the large oak tree in the middle of the graveyard, to do a little stargazing.

Chris and I are both interested in the UFO phenomena, and there is no better place to sky watch than in a dark location like Ridge Cemetery. It's amazing what you can see in this type of setting.

We sat our chairs up, so that Chris was facing the north, Janet was facing the south and I was facing the west.

Everything was quiet. We had been sitting for five minutes when Chris yelled out, *"Look at that!"*

"Look at what?" I asked. *"At that orange light, over there!"* He replied, pointing toward the north. *"It's above the treetops and descending into the woods."*

When I looked in the direction Chris was pointing, I saw nothing and neither did Janet.

"I don't see it, Chris," I replied.

"I think it landed in the woods over by the road," he added, raising his voice in excitement.

With that, we grabbed our chairs and loaded them in my vehicle, then walked down the road in search of the light.

The road is a half mile long, and is as dark if not darker than the graveyard. We walked the entire length of the road searching for the light but never saw it.

Chris described it as an orange shaped orb, about the size of a basketball.

"The light was just above the treetops and descending into the woods when I saw it," Chris said. *"It appeared to be under intelligent control like it was landing."*

The object he saw sounded similar to the orange light that the hunter witnessed. So, did they see the same thing only several years apart?

Confirmation from the Strangers

It took us forty-five minutes to make it down the road and back.

Unfortunately, we didn't encounter anything unusual, but hopefully the pair from Mattoon would be ready to leave when we got back.

We stopped at my vehicle for a drink of water, then headed back into the cemetery.

When we entered through the gate, it made a clanking sound that alerted the boy and his aunt we were back.

Immediately the boy came running toward us. As he approached us, he asked.

"Hey, have you guys seen anything yet?"

Still hoping that they would leave, I told another little white lie, even though Chris saw the orange light.

"No, we haven't seen anything all night," I replied.

"Oh boy, we have," he said excitedly.

"Really," I responded. *"What did you see?"*

"Well, we were over there in the far corner," he said, pointing toward the southeast corner of the graveyard by our base camp.

"I sat on the wooden bench next to the woods. When I did, I could feel someone standing behind me. So, I jumped up and turned around, but no one was there!"

"There seems to be something about that bench. I have had other people tell me the same thing," I responded to the boy.

"Then a few minutes later," he continued. "We were standing next to the timber in the corner, when suddenly, we heard something moving around in the woods. It sounded big," he exclaimed.

"We could see the trees and bushes moving, so we shined our flashlight where the movement was, but nothing was there, and the movement stopped."

"Tell them about the screaming voices," added his aunt.

"Screaming voices?" I thought to myself, thinking about the screams we heard earlier.

"Yeah, it was crazy," the boy added. "After the movement stopped, we were standing still listening and suddenly, we heard a group of people screaming. It was really faint, like it was coming from the woods! It lasted for a couple of minutes, then it stopped."

"Could you tell if it was a man or woman screaming?" I asked.

"It sounded like a bunch of people, men and women both, he replied.

"But you won't believe what else we saw," he added in an excited voice. "What did you see?" I questioned.

"Well," he said, pointing at the big oak tree in the center of the graveyard. *"We were walking toward that big tree when suddenly this neon green light came out of nowhere and was floating right in front of us."*

"How big was it?" I asked.

"It was the size of a softball," interjected the aunt.

"Yeah, it was weird," the boy added. *"This thing was going all over the place. Like a fish swimming in the water."*

"This is crazy," I thought to myself. *"They basically witnessed everything that we experienced tonight. The only exception was the light Chris saw, was orange, and what the boy and his aunt witnessed was neon green."*

After our conversation, the boy and his aunt decided it was getting late, so they finally headed home to Mattoon, leaving the graveyard for us to investigate.

Drumming and Chanting

It was nearing 2:00 A.M., but we still had a bit longer to investigate before packing up and heading home ourselves.

Everything was quiet until a few minutes before 3:00 A.M., when I heard something that at first, I thought was my mind playing tricks on me.

Out of the blue, I began hearing a faint rhythmic sound coming from the woods to the north of the parking area.

"Do you hear that?" I said to Chris and Janet. *Hear what?* Chris replied. *"I don't hear anything,"* added Janet. *"Listen, it's very faint. It sounds like someone is playing a tom-tom!"*

"Playing a tom-tom?" Chris questioned with a chuckle.

With that, everyone stood still, listening. After a few moments, Chris declared. *"I hear it! What the hell, it does sound like a tom-tom."*

Moments later, Janet heard it as well.

As we were listening to the drumming, suddenly we heard what sounded like Native American chanting.

The chanting was faint, like the drumming, but it was loud enough that we could hear it.

It was coming from the same direction as the rhythmic beat of the drum and we all heard it.

"Do you think maybe one of the locals is practicing some type of Native American ceremony?" Chris suggested.

"At Three-O'clock in the morning? I highly doubt it, Chris," I replied.

The drumming and chanting continued and was still going on when we left the cemetery after 3:30 A.M.

When we left, we didn't notice lights on in the homes of the residents living near the graveyard. So, Chris's theory that what we were hearing was one of the locals practicing some type of Native American ceremony seemed unlikely, unless they were practicing in the dark.

Later in the book, you will read about unexplained chanting I recorded during the Thrill at the Hill investigation, that may relate to the chanting heard July 10, 2010.

Stan and Belle

After our experiences on July 10th, Chris mentioned what we witnessed to longtime Bigfoot researcher Stan Courtney. Stan is well respected in the field of cryptozoology and considered one of the area's foremost experts on Bigfoot.

His research takes him all over the country, having been to many remote wilderness areas, conducting investigations.

He records the sounds of creatures of the night using sophisticated recording equipment.

Accompanying Stan on his investigations is his faithful companion Belle, a Karelian Bear Dog.

Chris told Stan about the movement in the woods and the walnut incident.

He was very interested in our encounter and explained that objects being thrown are often reported with Bigfoot activity. Some Bigfoot enthusiast believe they throw at intruders who wander into their territory as a way to remain hidden, while driving off the intruder.

A quick note regarding Stan and Bigfoot. Stan believes that Sasquatch, or Bigfoot, is a type of primate or undiscovered hominid or primitive creature.

Although Stan may be correct, my opinion differs from his. I believe these large, hairy creatures, which have been seen all over the world, are some type of interdimensional being that for whatever reason, can breach the veil between our world and theirs, allowing them to go back and forth between worlds.

One reason I believe this is there have been eyewitness reports of people seeing Bigfoot type creatures, described as being seven to eight feet tall and weighing six hundred pounds or more, who walk behind a tree or jump a fence and disappear.

It makes little sense that something that big can hide behind a tree. Nor does it make sense that large tracks are found in open areas. Then suddenly, the tracks stop, like the creature vanished into thin air.

Rather than hiding behind trees and vanishing into thin air, I believe they pass through some type of inter-dimensional doorway.

Native American legends, and religious texts like the Bible, speak of giants roaming the earth. So, possibly Bigfoot creatures are the giants referred to in the legends and text.

After talking to Stan, Chris called me and indicated that Stan wanted to investigate and set up recording equipment in the timber surrounding Ridge Cemetery. So, we scheduled an investigation with Stan for the following Saturday night.

The night of the investigation, Chris, a local paranormal investigator named Dan, and I met Stan and his dog Belle at Williamsburg Hill.

It was not a particularly active night, but something in or around the cemetery seemed to affect Belle.

According to Stan, Belle is a curious and fearless dog. She is trained not to bark when accompanying him on his investigations and loves exploring the woods, often straying away from him on her own. This information will be of importance as you continue reading.

We began the investigation at 10:00 P.M., by heading toward the southeast corner of the cemetery. This is the same corner that I threw the walnut into the woods, only to have it come flying back at us.

We were walking side by side, when I noticed Belle was walking behind me and was staying right on my heels.

I took a few steps to my left to look at something and Belle hurried behind me, again staying very close to me.

She stayed behind us the entire time that we were in this corner of the graveyard and didn't seem to be interested in exploring on her own.

If Belle were behind us and we moved, she would scurry to get behind us again. It seemed like something was scaring her.

This became so apparent that I mentioned Belle's odd behavior to the group.

Her actions puzzled Stan, and he explained how out of character this was for her.

"I have never seen her act like this," Stan explained. *"She has been in areas where bears and big cats live, and roams freely with no fear. She never acts like this."*

For whatever reason, there was something about the graveyard that Belle didn't like.

I wondered if whatever was alarming Belle was the same reason I have never seen wild animals in the cemetery?

Is there some unseen force in the graveyard that animal's sense and scares them away?

Based on the way Belle was reacting, if she had a choice, I don't think she would have been in the graveyard either.

While in the corner we pointed out to Stan where we encountered movement in the woods during the July 10 investigation and where the walnut was thrown.

The movement would not have been so interesting if it weren't for the fact when we shined our bright lights where the movement was occurring, nothing was there.

If a deer, big cat, or coyote, was nearby, we should have seen them.

From the corner of the graveyard, we followed the fence line around, toward the west.

We were nearing the cemetery entrance, when we heard something big moving in the woods, to the south of the gate.

Belle heard it too and moved toward the sound like she saw or sensed something in the woods.

She lowered her head and body like a bird dog on point, and began barking and growling, but Stan instructed her to be quiet.

Stan was perplexed by Belle's actions and mentioned this several times in the days following the investigation.

"I've never seen her react that way. It was totally out of character for her," Stan said.

He also told us that Belle seemed exhausted after the investigation, preferring to lie around rather than run and play as she normally did.

Using our flashlights, we searched the woods where the movement was coming from but saw nothing and the movement stopped.

Shortly after it stopped; Belle seemed more at ease. Later in the book, you will read interviews I conducted with a Logger and a hunter who witnessed something in the woods, that could be the culprit that roams the woods and possibly what Belle was sensing.

The Footprint

Later that night, we took a walk down the road. On our way back to the graveyard, Chris was walking along the edge of the timber, using his flashlight to see where he was going.

Suddenly he called out. *"Hey Larry, look at this!"* *"What did you find?"* I replied, noticing that he was kneeling down looking at something using the light from his flashlight.

"It's a footprint!" He answered.

"A footprint?" I questioned.

"Yeah, it's barefoot, you can see the toes, and look at the size of this thing!"

With that, we walked over to where Chris was kneeling to see what he found.

When I saw the footprint, it shocked me.

In the soft soil next to the woods, just as Chris said, was a large barefoot, footprint.

"That thing is huge," I said, placing my foot next to it for comparison.

I wear a size eleven and a half shoe, so in comparison, the footprint was fourteen or fifteen inches long and was barefoot, which made little sense.

No one in their right mind walks barefoot in the type of terrain that surrounds Ridge Cemetery. There are jagged rocks, thorns, poison ivy, beer cans and broken bottles to name a few of the hazards.

The footprint was in an inconspicuous place, so I don't think it was placed there by a prankster trying to fool someone. Chris found it by accident, so if it were some kind of joke, it would have been placed in an area it would have been easily found.

I started thinking about the stories I read, where people in several counties in Central Illinois, including Christian and

Macon counties, claim to have seen Bigfoot type creatures and have found large barefoot footprints.

Before I go any further, let me say this. I believe they exist, because there have been too many reports from credible witnesses claiming to have seen them.

If even one witness is correct about what they saw, then they are real.

What makes little sense is how they show up in places like Illinois, Indiana, and Missouri.

Even though these states have forested areas, if some undiscovered creature were roaming the woods, I would think one of the many thousands of hunters who frequent the woods in these areas, would have found substantial evidence of them, but they haven't.

So how is this possible?

I believe it goes back to my theory, that cryptids like Bigfoot, upright canines and the recent sightings of the Chicago Mothman are interdimensional or supernatural in nature, and somehow have access to our realm.

This would explain the accounts where people claim to see them running across roads and fields and simply disappear.

Was the footprint Chris found evidence of a Bigfoot creature roaming the woods near Ridge Cemetery? I am not sure, but it makes as much sense as someone running around barefoot in the rough, treacherous terrain in the wooded area near the cemetery, to play a joke.

What Opened the Box

At the end of the investigation, Stan placed two sophisticated audio recorders in the woods.

He puts the recorders in heavy grade military ammunition boxes that he has customized to protect the recorders from the elements.

He then places the boxes in strategic locations and leaves them for several days to record animal sounds and the sounds of anything else that might be roaming the woods.

One box was placed in the area where the walnut incident took place. He left the recorders for several days, then retrieved them and reviewed the recordings.

It was while reviewing audio from the recorder placed near the southeast corner of the graveyard, Stan heard something that to this day he cannot explain.

The lid of the boxes fit snug, so in order to open them, it takes two hands. You have to pull up on the latch with one hand and steady the box with the other.

The recorders Stan uses can record sounds hundreds of feet away. When Stan listened to the recording, he could hear the latch of the box being lifted, then opening. Moments later, it slammed shut.

Stan was baffled that no footsteps or movement, caused by an animal or a person approaching the box before it opened, were recorded.

With all the dried leaves and branches on the ground, he should have recorded whatever it was approaching the box, but he didn't.

Nor did he record the sound of an approaching vehicle on the gravel road pulling up to the cemetery.

"I recorded only the sound of the box opening and slamming shut, which makes no sense," Stan said.

Stan, a very logical and analytical investigator, was baffled by how anything could get close enough to the box to open it, without being heard and their movements recorded.

"It really has me scratching my head," Stan told me. *"An animal can't open the box because you have to have thumbs to open the latch. Plus, whether it was an animal or a person, I should have recorded them approaching the box, but I didn't."*

The Thrill at the Hill Investigation
September 28, 2012

Along the way on my journey and adventure into the world of the unexplained, I have met many people, and made some great new friends. One friend hosts a local morning radio show on 99.7 THE MIX in Springfield, Illinois, called *The Morning Grind*.

The host of the show is Jason Bond, better known by his on-air name, *"Bondsy."* I met him in October 2011, when the radio station was known as 99.7 KISS FM. He invited me to be on their show, to talk about the paranormal and share a few of the experiences I had as a paranormal investigator.

After telling several stories, it wasn't that Bondsy didn't believe me, but he is skeptical about such things by nature and wanted to see if the paranormal was real for himself. So, I invited him to tagalong on a few investigations, and as they say, the rest is history.

Since 2011, 99.7 KISS FM, now 99.7 THE MIX, does a live Halloween show that airs on Halloween morning which I co-host with him.

For the 2012 show, Bondsy suggested doing an investigation prior to Halloween, pre-record it, then do a live on-air recap, Halloween morning. Since 2012, Bondsy has been on nine investigations with me.

He asked me if I knew of a haunted location that would make for a good show, so I told him about the activity that takes place at Ridge Cemetery at Williamsburg Hill, and some of my personal experiences there.

After hearing about my experiences, he decided that Ridge Cemetery would be a perfect location to record the show. Little did we know that an electronic device I had never used in a cemetery before, would get the attention of all involved and steal the show!

Several days before our adventure, I contacted Bondsy to coordinate the details of the investigation, such as who was going with us and when and where I would pick them up.

We decided that his co-host, Sarah and intern Taylor Fishburn, whose on-air nickname is Tuna-melt, or Tuna for short, would accompany us on our quest for ghost. You will see the importance of Taylor's nickname to the investigation as you continue reading.

The plan was for me to pick up Sarah and Taylor at the station. Bondsy would be running late because of a family commitment, so he would meet us at the local JC Penny parking lot in Springfield and we would leave from there to make the fifty-mile trek to Williamsburg Hill.

While coordinating our plans, I mentioned to Bondsy I wanted to conduct an experiment with Sarah and Tuna-melt. I told him about the boy's grave and how women become emotional when near it. I explained the importance of the girls not knowing what to expect, because from past experience, it seemed the reaction of women had to be spontaneous.

Although Sarah had been with me on two prior investigations, this would be Bondsy and Tuna's first paranormal adventure.

When I picked the girls up at the station, Sarah asked me to tell Tuna a few stories about my paranormal encounters over the years. I'm not sure if this was a good idea, because with each story I told, Tuna became more and more un-nerved about the night's investigation.

Bondsy arrived at 9:00 P.M., and we headed to Williamsburg Hill for our paranormal adventure.

We stopped at a convenience store in Tower Hill, to pick up drinks and snacks, then made the final trek from Tower Hill to our destination.

It was an overcast night and the closer we got to Williamsburg Hill, the darker it became.

I turned onto Road 1100 East and followed the winding road to the top of the Hill. As we neared the graveyard; the more anxious Tuna became.

Williamsburg Hill is beautiful during the daytime, but at night, it can be a frightening place.

At the top of the hill, we turned left at the tall microwave tower and headed down the narrow road leading to the graveyard. We didn't get far when a nervous sounding Tuna yelled out.

"Stop the car, I'm going to get sick!"

She was so scared that she was literally getting sick to her stomach. It didn't help matters that my CD player was playing the theme song from the movie Halloween!

Tuna was legitimately nervous and sick to her stomach, so I muted the music and pulled over.

We waited for a couple of minutes, until the sick feeling Tuna had subsided, then continued our journey down the narrow gravel road which dead ended at the cemetery gate.

My headlights lit up the spooky graveyard under the pallid moon, a frigid wind rustling the brown leaves, making the perfect setting for ghouls, goblins, and ghost.

The way the road dead-ends the cemetery appears out of nowhere, giving off an eerie feeling that someone or something is waiting for the next visitor.

During the nighttime, especially on overcast nights or when there is a new moon, Ridge Cemetery, is one of the darkest places I have ever investigated. I have spent several nights out here alone, and without fail, have had the feeling I was being watched and followed. If you want a genuine thrill, venture out to this place alone some night.

As we pulled in, I made a U-turn and parked so that my vehicle was facing the direction I had just come from. I always do this but am not sure why. Maybe it's easier to unload equipment, or maybe it's in case I see something so terrifying I need to make a quick getaway.

We exited the vehicle and although I don't remember which one said it, one of the girls commented they couldn't believe how dark it was.

The only sound was a steady and at times, strong breeze. It was a cool, but not cold night.

For the investigation, we would use digital audio recorders and a video camera. But the most important piece of equipment on this night would turn out to be a device called an *SB-7 Spirit box*.

The SB-7 is a mini AM-FM frequency sweeper. Or basically it is a radio that has been altered to continuously scan either the AM or FM radio frequencies. It sweeps in milliseconds and can be set to sweep either forward or backward.

Originally, I didn't buy into the idea of the box working. I believed the voices coming through were nothing more than radio skip combined with a phenomenon called audio pareidolia. Audio pareidolia is simply our mind matrixing or trying to associate the sounds coming through the box with words familiar to us.

But I soon changed my mind, because I not only heard words coming through, but heard complete sentences as well, which was not possible based on the speed the frequencies are scanned, which is 100 milliseconds per second. Plus, many times, what came through were answers to questions I asked or were names and things associated with the location I was investigating.

The puzzling thing about the box is that on some nights, it is totally useless, while other nights, the most amazing communication comes through.

Now any time that I use the SB-7 box, I record the session because for some reason it is easier to hear and understand the voices that come through. Plus, I have recorded proof of what was said.

As you continue reading, you will see how the box also convinced the radio crew it works.

We carried the equipment to the southeast corner of the graveyard and set up our base camp for the night. I have investigated Ridge Cemetery well over one-hundred times and as I have mentioned previously, without any doubt, most of the activity seems to take place in this area.

Although we didn't realize it until a few days later when we reviewed our audio evidence, we recorded a strange, clear voice that did not belong to any of us. The voice was recorded soon after we set up our base camp.

Based on what was said, it seemed to interact with us, or at least knew the name of one of the team members. The voice was recorded near the grave of the young boy, and I have often wondered if it was his voice that we recorded.

At the time, Bondsy was recording a segment for the Halloween show using an audio recorder belonging to the station. Sarah and I were nearby setting up equipment and Tunamelt was checking out a grave.

Before I describe what took place, I should explain the good-natured arguing that takes place between Bondsy and Sarah, both on the radio and in their personal friendship. I compare it to arguing between a brother and sister.

As Bondsy was recording the sound bite for the show, he looked at Sarah and said, *"Have you guys seen anything yet?"*

Sarah, who was more unnerved by the thought of coyotes

or possibly drug dealers showing up, than worried about ghost or spirits, gave Bondsy a worried look, and said nothing.

Immediately, Bondsy said, *"Ok, you two city broads need to calm down!"* Referring to Sarah and Tuna! Sarah fired back by saying, *"OK, Mr. St. Louis,"* insinuating Bondsy, who had grown up in St. Louis, Missouri was no outdoorsman.

Bondsy replied by saying, *"Where do I live?"* To which Sarah replies, *"You live on a numbered street!"*

Unbeknownst to us at the time, as soon as Sarah replies, *"You live on a numbered street,"* a voice comes out of nowhere that was not one of us, nor did we hear it, but was recorded.

The voice sounds like an adolescent male and is loud and clear. Who, or whatever it was, was close to the recorder which was in Bondsy's hand. So, if they were close to the recorder, they were close to us as well.

What is said is a voice clearly saying, *"I feel Sarah!"*

The voice saying Sarah's name is confirmation for me that who or whatever was there that night, was intelligent and must have been listening to our conversations, because it knew our names.

We did not hear the voice, so following Bondsy and Sarah's brief exchange, Sarah and I walked back to my vehicle to get my reading glasses, which I had left on the front seat of my vehicle. When we returned, I decided it would be a good time to conduct our first SB-7 Spirit Box session of the night.

I had used the box many times before, but never used it in a graveyard, so I wasn't sure what to expect.

We conducted the session at our base camp, near the gravesite of the young man. Sarah and Tunamelt were seated in camping chairs, and Bondsy was seated on a wooden bench next to the edge of the cemetery, near the timber.

The reason that he wanted to sit on the bench was earlier in the evening, I told him how during the summer of 2010, investigator Chris sat on the bench, and after a short time, jumped off claiming it felt like someone was standing behind him.

Sarah was the only member of the group who had seen the SB-7 box in action before. Bondsy had heard me talk about it and how I had heard strange voices come through the box.

Being the skeptic he is, he wanted to see the box in action for himself before believing that it worked.

If you have never heard one of the boxes in use, you primarily hear static and white noise, with an occasional word come through. The box scans the radio frequencies in milliseconds; so whole words and statements should not have time to come through.

Using the box many times over the last several years, I have asked questions relevant to particular investigations, and received responses pertinent to the location. I have also asked questions, such as, *"Who is the president of the United States?"* In 2014, when asking this question, I received three simultaneous answers come through within seconds of each other, in different voices, genders, and on different frequencies, all saying the same thing, *"Obama!"*

On another occasion, shortly after an investigator turned the box on, a clear voice came through that said, *"Shame on Chris!"*

Chris was the name of the investigator who turned on the box.

The words, *"Shame on Chris"* sounded like the same voice, but came through on different frequencies, which rules out radio skip.

If I had to choose a particular word to come through the box during the KISS FM investigation that would convince Bondsy, Sarah and Taylor that the SB-7 spirit box works, I couldn't have planned it any better.

As we were listening to the annoying static coming through the device, out of the blue, a loud and clear voice said, *"Tuna!"*

Immediately Taylor said, *"Did that just say my name?"*

Sarah quickly responded with a disbelieving, *"What!"* Bondsy responded in a more colorful manner by saying *"Holy Shit!"* We all heard what was said. It clearly said *"Tuna!"* It was unbelievable.

The voice was male, and as remarkable and unbelievable as this was, it was only the beginning. Because, throughout the night, each time we did a box session, a clear voice came through that said *"Tuna."* During some of the sessions, *"Tuna"* was said more than once.

One comment made by Bondsy that night, stuck with me as confirmation he believes the box works.

The comment Bondsy made was after we heard Tuna's name come through the box several more times.

Bondsy said. *"Man, this makes little sense! Hearing the name Tuna, which is the nickname of one of the people who was with us, coming through a radio box scanning multiple frequencies, in the middle of the night, in a cemetery, located out in the middle of nowhere, doesn't make sense! Unless someone is out here doing a freaking Chicken of the Sea commercial for Tuna, you shouldn't get that word coming through a radio box!"*

Well, I'm fairly certain, there was no one doing a Chicken

of the Sea commercial at Williamsburg Hill, so I'm pretty sure we can rule that out as a possibility of who said Tuna's name.

We heard the word Tuna come through multiple times, so at one point, I asked Taylor if she would mind holding the box as a test of sorts to see what would happen. She said she didn't mind, so I handed her the box. As soon as I placed it in her hands, once again, a clear male voice said, *"Tuna!"*

We were amazed at what we were hearing. Because it made little sense.

Since whom or whatever the voice was, seemed to focus on Taylor, I asked her if anyone close to her had passed away recently. She said that her grandfather, on her mother's side, passed away recently, and that she was close to him.

Taylor explained that her grandfather was known by his nickname, *Dandy!*

I asked Taylor to ask a question that only her grandfather would know the answer to. She thought about it for a moment, and then she said. *"Grand-pa Dandy, this is Taylor, can you tell me what color my hair was when I was a little girl?"*

Within moments *a* male voice came through and said. *"Red!"*

We all heard the voice as Taylor responded. *"No way! Until I was seven years old, I had red hair! Grand-Pa Dandy would definitely have known that!"*

From the look on Taylor's face, and the tone of her voice, I could tell she was starting to believe that; maybe this was Grand-Pa Dandy, communicating with her.

Tuna asked several more questions, but we couldn't understand any of the responses.

Since the voices coming through seemed to have stopped, I decided we should turn the box off for a while. I asked Taylor to announce to Grand-Pa Dandy, that we were going to turn the box off, and ask him if he had anything else, he wanted to say before we did.

So, Taylor said aloud, *"Grand-Pa-Dandy, we are going to turn the box off, is there anything else you want to say?"*

Within moments, a clear male voice came through that said, *"Stay!"* Was this Tuna's grandfather, and did he want her to stay and talk to him a bit longer?

After we finished the SB-7 box session, I decided to move one of my audio recorders to a different location.

While Bondsy, Sarah and Tunamelt, remained near the base camp, I walked back toward the big oak tree in the center of the cemetery. Twenty yards past the tree is a clearing where there are no headstones.

For the longest time, I couldn't figure out why no one was buried there, because it was the nicest location in the cemetery. Then one day, I spoke to a resident of Williamsburg Hill, who told me that Native Americans are buried there. He said stones were used to cover the graves but over the years; soil erosion has occurred and covered the stones.

Even before I found out that Native Americans were buried there, there was something odd about this part of the cemetery. At times it is much cooler than the rest of the graveyard, which made little sense, because there are no trees to shade the area.

Occasionally, when near the graves, I have felt the presence of someone nearby watching me.

After walking across the cemetery, I placed the audio recorder near a grave marker a few feet from the Native

American graves. After placing the recorder, I returned to the group to continue the investigation.

Nothing unusual happened, nor did I hear anything during the investigation. But a few days later, when I reviewed the audio from the recorder, I discovered I had recorded an EVP.

It is one of the most amazing and pertinent pieces of evidence validating paranormal activity that I have ever recorded.

The EVP was not just your standard disembodied voice, but sounded like Native American chanting.

What I recorded sounds like someone is chanting, *"Ye-ya-he-he!"* It is definitely chanting or singing. Before and after the chant is a single human sounding whistle.

We didn't hear the chant or whistling during the investigation, but it is evidence like this that keeps me coming back for more of what the supernatural has to offer!

Recording chanting next to the graves of Native Americans makes it hard to dispute that spirits of Indians still roam Williamsburg Hill.

Earlier in the book, I mentioned trying the experiment at the boy's grave with the girls. At one point, Sarah walked in front of the grave, so I asked her to stop. I told her I wanted to try something and asked her to stand in front of the grave, then tell me how she felt.

When I asked her how she felt, she said, *"I don't feel anything!"*

"You don't feel anything?" I questioned.

"No, nothing at all," she replied.

I asked Sarah to move away, then asked Taylor to stand next to the grave!

Immediately without prompting, she said, *"I don't know what it is, but I'm doing all I can to keep from getting emotional!"*

The boy's grave seemed to have an additional effect on Taylor, besides causing her to become emotional.

I say this, because when we first arrived at the graveyard, she was uneasy about being in a haunted cemetery, and was on edge like Sarah.

Later she told me that after standing next to the boys' grave and becoming emotional; her fears subsided, and she felt comforted.

As she was telling me this, I wondered if the voice coming through the box really was her grandfather. If so, maybe it was his presence rather than her emotional reaction to the grave that calmed her fears. No matter what happened, something comforted Taylor that night!

While reviewing additional audio, Bondsy found a second EVP he recorded near the boys' grave. It was captured on the audio recorder he brought from the station.

When he first heard the voice, he almost ignored it, thinking it was some kind of electronic interference that caused one of our voices to be distorted.

What was unusual about the recording is it sounded mechanical. I can best describe it as a *"Darth Vader"* type voice from the movie Star Wars!

Bondsy played the recording for one of the radio station's technicians, who has recorded hours and hours of audio, and was familiar with the recorder Bondsy used.

The technician did not understand what could have caused the distortion, since others were talking before and after the voice. So, if one voice was distorted, all of our voices should have been, but they weren't.

Bondsy emailed the EVP to me, but I still couldn't understand what was being said. For that matter, none of us could.

When I arrived the morning of the Halloween show, I didn't realize that Bondsy had edited the clip using professional grade audio editing software. He slowed the clip down a bit and removed background noise for better clarity.

When it came time to play the clip, he explained to me on air that after he last talked to me; he edited the clip and after doing so, could understand what was being said and believed that I would too.

To my disappointment, when he played it, I still couldn't determine what it was saying. Then during a commercial break, I told Bondsy that it sounded like it was going too fast and needed to be slowed down a bit more.

So, he re-edited the clip, slowed it down, then played it back for me. When he did, even though it sounded like a mechanical voice, I could tell what was being said.

The voice seemed to be answering a question another spirit asked. But there was no doubt that the voice was clearly saying, *"That's Larry's Girl!"*

When I heard the voice, I immediately thought about what a legit psychic named Cheryl told me several years before.

I had been prompted to go see her by several co-workers and friends in my office. They all marveled at how gifted she was, so I made an appointment for a reading.

When I arrived that day, she told me she got her gift of clairvoyance after having a near death experience in which she saw a Native American spirit named Shirocka, pronounced, "Sure-rock-a." When she told me this, I thought to myself, *"Larry, what did you get yourself into?"*

But by the time I left her home that day, I was dumbfounded and completely blown away by her gift of clairvoyance.

This lady didn't know me, yet she knew everything about me.

As I was getting ready to leave and we were saying our goodbyes, Cheryl asked me to sit down again, because Shirocka had another message for me.

The psychic said, *"Larry, Shirocka says you have two children." "No,"* I replied, *"I have one child, a son."*

"Shirocka says you have a little girl, an angel baby." Then it hit me, and I knew exactly what Shirocka was talking about.

In 1997, my wife and I lost a child during my wife's pregnancy. We lost her late term, so we named her Kari Rene and had a private burial service for her.

The psychic continued and told me the following.

"Shirocka wants you to know that before we are born into the physical world, we choose our parents, and your angel baby chose you and your wife as her father and mother. But before she was born, an important task was presented to her, and she made the unselfish decision to stay in the spirit world, so she could not come to be with you in the physical world. But she loves you and her mother very much and is always with you. Larry, Shirocka tells me that sometimes you feel your angel baby around you. That you feel a presence of someone that you can't explain. This is your

angel baby."

What the psychic said was true because I had this feeling many times. There was no way she could have known any of the things about me she knew that day, but she did. So, I had to believe that Kari Rene was around as well.

After Bondsy played the clip, and I heard the, *"That's Larry's girl,"* voice, I looked at Bondsy. He knows the story of our daughter's death and of my experiences with the psychic. "Bondsy," I said! *"What if the psychic was right when she said my daughter is always with me! What if she was with me in the cemetery that night and a spirit didn't recognize her and asked another spirit? Who is that? And the spirit answered, that's Larry's girl!"*

Bondsy looked at me and said, *"Dude, that's exactly what I was thinking. When I heard the voice, I wanted to say something, but I didn't know how you might feel about it!"*

Is it possible that the spirit of my little girl was in Ridge Cemetery that night, or is it wishful thinking on my part? There is no way I can prove she was in the graveyard, but I know one thing. She is always with me, in my heart!

There were several unusual experiences during the Thrill at the Hill investigation, most of which was focused on Taylor. But why her, especially at a location she had never been to before?

This is another question that will probably go unanswered, and a question that adds to the strangeness and mystery of Williamsburg Hill!

The day after our investigation, Taylor sent a private Facebook message to me. I think she sent the message because she was confused by what happened. If you think about it, she had never been on a paranormal investigation and probably figured nothing would happen. Then suddenly and totally unexpected by her, she experiences something you would expect to read in a Stephen King novel.

Imagine hearing your nickname called out over a radio receiver in the middle of the night in a secluded graveyard.

Even I was skeptical of the SB-7 box before I used it, but there is nothing like seeing the unexplained firsthand to make a believer out of you, and I think in Taylor, Bondsy and Sarah's case, it has!

If Taylors nickname were a common name like Mary or Sue, it would be easier to write off as radio skip or coincidence. But a name like Tuna causes one to scratch their head. Plus, not only did we hear the name come through, but heard and recorded it nine times.

In her message, Taylor told me she had pondered whether to tell her mother, Lindsey, about going on a paranormal investigation and the strange experiences she had. How a voice came through a simple radio device that knew her nickname, and called it out not once, but many times. Or how it answered a specific question she asked about the color of her hair when she was a little girl. Taylor was even more hesitant to bring up the possibility that the voice may have been her grandfather Dandy, who is her mother's father!

Finally, Taylor told her mother about her bizarre experiences at the graveyard, including becoming emotional as she stood by the boy's grave.

When she told her mother, she had asked about the color of her hair when she was a little girl, and a voice coming through the box responded with the correct answer. She asked her mother if she thought Dandy is the type of person who would try to communicate with the living after death.

It shocked Taylor, when her mother told her she had recently gone to see a clairvoyant and had discussed her grandfather with the psychic.

One thing that the psychic told her mother was that her father was around all the time.

"So yes, Taylor," her mother said. *"I definitely believe that Grand-pa Dandy would try to contact his granddaughter through a radio device, if he had the opportunity to."*

Then Taylors mother said to her. *"I'm not sure if you realize this, but last night when you were in the cemetery, was your Grandfather's birthday!"*

When I read that the night of our investigation was her grandfather's birthday, an icy chill ran down my spine. Because after all, what were the odds?

I am not sure if Bondsy and the crew from the radio station found the proof they were looking for to decide if the paranormal is real. But I can say with certainty the events that took place on September 28, 2012, are one's none of us will soon forget.

The most puzzling aspect of the voice coming through the box is why did it call out Taylor's nickname instead of her given name? Unfortunately, we may never know the answer in this lifetime.

Most who live in Shelby County in Illinois, have heard the stories that have made the legend of Williamsburg Hill's Ridge Cemetery what it is today.

To some it is just a graveyard, to others it is a frightening place. To me, it is a location where strange things happen and a place I hope to explore for a long time to come.

Canadian author Robertson Davies once said, *"The eyes see only what the mind is prepared to comprehend."* Well, it is a safe bet to say that Mr. Davies never visited Williamsburg

Hills Ridge Cemetery, a place that is a veritable paranormal stew of unexplained activity that many have witnessed.

Hopefully, I will be lucky enough to see more of what it offers and solve some of the mystery that makes it such a strange place.

But if I don't, I can truly say I have seen and experienced enough of the strangeness that goes on to label the place haunted.

Watcher in the Woods

There were many times during my investigations at Ridge Cemetery, I felt that eyes were watching me from the woods.

You have read about my encounter with the eerie whistling that was beckoning me to come into the dark timber and how uncharacteristically, Stan Courtney's dog Belle, reacted to something roaming about the woods. You also read about tree's and large limbs appearing out of nowhere, blocking the only exit from the graveyard.

For years, I have wondered if it isn't a human carrying out these deeds, what type of creature or being could do these things without being seen.

Well, the answer to this question may come from logger Scott Turley's recent encounter in the summer of 2020.

As I was writing this book, I received a message from the editor of the Pana News Palladium John Broux, who wanted to know if I had any stories in the Shelbyville, Pana Illinois areas he could use for their Halloween addition. I told him I was in the process of finishing a book about the strange goings on at Williamsburg Hill.

So, I sent him an excerpt from the book to use, and at the end of my article, I included a note, that if anyone had their own experience at Williamsburg Hill, I would like to hear from them and included my contact information.

Adding the note at the end of the article proved to be more fruitful than I ever expected, because as a result of it, several eyewitnesses were made known to me.

The day after the article was published, I received a message from a lady named Natasha, who indicated she read the article and thought I would be interested in hearing about a recent encounter that her Father, Scott Turley had.

Where Scott's story differs from the others, is that he not only felt he was being watched, but he also saw the creature that was watching him, as well.

Natasha provided her Dad's phone number, so I called him. Little did I expect the fascinating and chilling story I was about to hear.

Scott explained to me that he is a logger by trade and spends a lot of time in the woods. He told me he is not the type of person who gets spooked easily and tries to dismiss stories about the goings on at places like Williamsburg Hill, unless he sees them for himself, which is exactly what happened in the summer of 2020.

The incident took place on a hot day in the woods east of Ridge Cemetery. It was midday during the last week of July or the first week of August. Scott had cut trees in the same area the year before, and on this day had been cutting and hauling trees out on skid roads laid out by the logging crew.

Scott told me that the previous year, his two co-workers had played pranks on each other, so he expected similar behavior from the two this year as well.

When the incident took place, Scott was driving a skid-loader, which is a four-wheel-drive tractor with a grapple on one end, used to drag cut logs. As he was driving the loader, something caught his eye, so he turned and looked.

When he did, he saw someone or something look around both sides of a tree, then peek its head out, watching him as he drove through.

"My first thought was it was one of the sons of the guy I was working for trying to play a prank on me, but as far as I knew, they hadn't arrived for work yet," Scott said.

"Not taking my eye off of the figure, I reached down and turned the machine off, and yelled, hey! As soon as I shut off the machine, this thing ducked back behind the tree so I couldn't see it. What was really odd, was it ducked back so fast it was like a blur, and a person couldn't move that fast."

"Giggling, still thinking it was one of the guys, I jumped off the machine and walked toward the tree. When I got to the tree and popped around the other side, I was laughing and hollered, got ya! But there was nobody there."

"I walked around the tree a half a dozen times, looking up and looking down. There was nothing in the tree and there was nothing in the woods, whatever was there vanished into thin air."

Scott told me that he is in his mid-fifties and doesn't spook easily, but what he saw really shook him up.

He described the being as someone or something wearing a black hoodie pulled up over their head. He couldn't make out a face but could see black hands on either side of the tree that were grasping it.

"Whatever this thing was, had to be at least seven feet tall," he said. *"Because the seat I was sitting in, was four or five feet off the ground, and where the face of this thing would be,*

was eye-level with me. It just peeked around the tree like it was watching me."

Scott told me that the temperature was in the nineties so he couldn't imagine anyone would be wearing a hoodie on such a hot summer day.

When Scott realized there was no one there, he went back to the skid-loader and climbed into the seat and thought about what he saw.

Try as he may, he couldn't rationalize what he saw. *"Not much bothers me,"* he said. *"But seeing a hooded figure peeking around a tree then vanish into thin air, shook me up a bit."*

So, what did Scott see? Was it a ghost or some type of ghoul capable of vanishing into thin air? Is what he witnessed the source of the strange whistling I heard or the culprit who places logs across the road trapping unsuspecting visitors to the graveyard? We may never know, but for Scott Turley, it is something that he won't soon forget!

After interviewing Scott, I ran across a post by the moderator of a paranormal consortium in Springfield, Illinois that I am a member of, the Prairieland Paranormal Consortium.

The consortium is moderated by Carl Jones, a friend and paranormal colleague, who I mentioned earlier in the book, and whose story of a paranormal experience he had as a teenager, is featured in the Campfire Tales, portion of this book.

What caught my attention was an interview Carl recently conducted with a woman from the Charleston-Mattoon, Illinois area, who witnessed something similar to what Scott saw.

So, I contacted Carl, who provided the name and phone number of the witness's sister, Nancy, who in turn, put me in contact with her sister the witness, Margaret Botts.

As you read my interview with Margaret, you will see the similarities to what Scott witnessed.

Not only is the description of what she saw, similar, but the Charleston-Mattoon area is only fifty miles from Williamsburg Hill, so it is entirely plausible that such a creature could have migrated to the Williamsburg Hill area.

My interview was conducted by phone, since Margaret now lives in Montana where she runs a hotel. Based on my interview, I believe her to be a very credible and convincing witness.

(Margaret's Interview)

"I don't recall if it was September or October, but it was the fall of 2012, and was early morning. It was sometime before 5:00 A.M., still dark and a light misty rain was falling. I was on my way to work at Sarah Bush Lincoln Hospital, which is located on Route 16 between Charleston and Mattoon. I was only a short distance from the highway and was driving on road 1200 East. There are several big hills along the road before you get to the highway, and I had just reached the top of the last big hill. So, all that was left was the short straightaway before reaching Route 16, which was only a half-mile away."

"When I got to the top of the hill, off to the side, I saw something coming out from a driveway directly to the east. There are five or six homes in the area, and it was coming from between two of them. Most of the houses are very close to the road, but the yard it was coming from was a bit further back, so I couldn't see it very well at first. Then it moved to the edge of the road, and I could clearly see that it was some type of creature or being, that was seven to eight feet tall,

dark black, solid looking and was wearing a black cloak with a black hood. It never looked at me the entire time I saw it."

"It was upright, and as soon as it got to the road, it moved forward to cross the road, but instead of walking or running, it jumped to move. Even stranger, each time it jumped, it jumped about three feet in the air and jumped so fast that it could not have been a human. It moved slowly forward because it had to jump so many times to get across the road. It was moving vertically so fast it was like a blur and its knees never bent when it jumped up or down. The cloak it had on, was long and went all the way to the ground, so I couldn't tell if it had legs or not. But the way the cloak was shaped, it looked like it may have had wings or something under it. It sort of reminded me of the John Travolta movie, Michael, and how Michael would wear a long coat to hide his wings. I'm not saying it had wings, but it looked like there may have been something under the cloak."

"This thing continued to jump until it made it across the road. I stopped my car to avoid hitting it, and it was only twenty-five feet from me. My headlights lit it up all the way across the road, so I got a real good look at it. When it made it across the road, I watched it until it disappeared into the darkness of a wooded area."

"Like I said, it never looked at me, so I have no idea if it knew I was there or not."

The description of what Margaret saw is similar to the creature Scott witnessed peeking around the tree this summer.

Her sighting was in 2012, so it would not be out of the question, that the Coles County creature could have made its way to the woods of Williamsburg Hill in eight years.

If it had wings like she suspected, there is no question that such a creature could have migrated to Shelby County. Or is it possible, there are more than one of the creatures milling about Central Illinois.

After interviewing Scott and Margaret, I decided to dig a bit deeper and look for additional witnesses, which led me to a hunter who has been hunting in the woods that surround Ridge Cemetery for over twenty years.

To say that he has had some strange and frightening experiences would be a major understatement. Plus, he too, has seen a creature similar to what Scott Turley witnessed, not once but several times.

The hunter was okay with me using his stories for the book, but preferred to remain anonymous, so I will simply call him Mr. Smith, in order to keep his identity private.

The Hunter

I was given the name and phone number of the hunter, by one of the many witnesses I interviewed for the writing of this book. He told me that he had known Smith for many years and considered him to be a hardworking, no non-sense type of guy.

The witness told me that Smith had hunted in the woods of Williamsburg Hill for many years and had seen and experienced some very strange things while in the woods.

After playing phone tag for better than a week, Smith called me on a Thursday evening and our conversation lasted over an hour and a half. The length of our conversation was due to all the strange things that had happened to him while hunting in the woods near Ridge Cemetery.

It was also during the interview, that I found out that the area where Smith has had his encounters, is the same area that Scott Turley witnessed the black hooded figure.

"It's just weird up here," he told me. "Anything and everything happens on the hill."

"I have been hunting up here for over twenty years and I know the woods like the back of my hand. Plus, you're not talking about a national forest, but a parcel of land that is less than twenty acres. There is a path that starts at the edge of the woods, that is a short ten-minute walk to a tree-stand that I use for hunting."

"I have walked to the tree-stand hundreds of times, and don't even need a flashlight to find it at night, because I know exactly where it is. Following the path, you walk up and down several gulley's, and the stand is just past one of the gulley's. But there have been several times, that I became totally lost and had no clue where I was. It happened three times in one year and one time it was during the daytime. It didn't make any sense."

Mr. Smith told me that, the times that this has happened, it seemed like his walk to the tree stand took forever, and he didn't recognize where he was.

"I kept thinking; this is taking forever. It wasn't like I was going through brush or anything, so I knew I wasn't walking in a circle. I was walking straight down the path, then the next thing I knew, I was lost," he said. "It didn't make sense! There is no way it should have taken so long to walk to the tree stand."

"I would get so lost, that I would have to sit down and wait for daybreak. When the sun would rise, I would realize that I was sitting under the tall microwave tower at the top of the hill over four-hundred yards from the tree-stand. Plus, from my property to the tower is only a fifteen-minute walk and it would take at least thirty minutes or more to the spot I would finally give up and sit down until daylight."

"But the weirdest thing was when I got lost in the daytime

around noon. There is no way, I should have got lost at all, let alone get lost in broad daylight. Somehow, I became disoriented and completely lost and like I said, the tree-stand is a straight shot, down the path. It wasn't until I reached the microwave tower, that I finally realized where I was at."

If getting lost in an area familiar to him wasn't strange enough, what he was about to tell me next, sent an icy chill down my back.

"I usually head out early in the morning to go hunting. Most times its several hours before sunrise. Numerous times, while sitting in my tree-stand, I have heard voices. The frightening thing about the voices is, they don't come from the ground level, but from right in front of my face, and the tree-stand I am sitting in, is ten feet off the ground."

Even though I was interviewing Mr. Smith over the phone, I could tell by the tone of his voice that hearing the voices were disturbing to him.

"Most of the voices are men's voices, but I have heard a woman speaking as well," he said.

"On two occasions, I could understand what the voices were saying. Once I heard a woman clearly say, (Come,) followed by several other words that I couldn't make out. On another occasion, it was around 4:00 A.M., I was quietly sitting in the tree-stand, when I heard a man's voice, that sounded like he was right in front of my face, say, (Great weather we are having.) What he said, may not sound threatening, but when you are sitting ten feet up in a tree and a voice speaks to you right in front of your face, it tends to frighten you."

The voice unnerved smith so much that he waited until sunrise to climb down from the tree, then left the woods for the day.

Smith told me that the man spoke with what sounded like a British or European accent.

Smith also told me that while camping out, he has heard muffled voices of men and women screaming. *"The voices are faint, but you can hear them,"* he said.

If you will recall from a bit earlier in the book, during one of my investigations, my investigative team and I heard the sound of muffled screams in the southeast corner of the graveyard.

In addition to hearing the voices, Smith has also seen things watching him while he is sitting in the tree stand.

"It's happened a lot," he said. *"I'll be sitting in the stand waiting for a deer to come by and I will see these black hooded figures, peeking around trees across from me. At first, I thought it was someone messing around, so I would call out, (Hey what are you doing?) But whatever these things are, they would just duck back behind the tree and disappear."*

I asked Smith how tall the beings were, and he said he couldn't tell for sure, but they are very tall. *"When I have seen them, they are eye level to me and like I said, I am ten feet up the tree sitting in a tree-stand."*

Smith described the beings as being all black and wearing black hoods. He has seen them both in the daytime and at night and has seen them for years.

I told him about what logger Scott Turley witnessed and Smith indicated that he knows Scott, and what the logger saw, sounds exactly like what he has witnessed.

If you will recall, earlier in the book, I mentioned the lack of small animals in and around Ridge Cemetery. So, during our phone conversation, I mentioned this to Mr. Smith, and he too indicated that he has noticed this, and does not have an explanation for it, unless, there is some type of big cat, like a cougar or panther, which has long been rumored to roam Williamsburg Hill, feeding on them.

But with that being said, he told me that he has never found tracks belonging to such a creature and as much time as he has spent in the woods, hunting the area, he should have found tracks if they were living on the hill.

He did say that with all the gulley's and thick underbrush, it is highly possible they could remain hidden.

From research on big cats that I did for the book, I found that they are territorial, so it is not uncommon that one lone cat stalks an area. If this is the case on Williamsburg Hill, then it is plausible that a big cat could roam the hill and remain undetected, feeding on small animals.

At the conclusion of our interview, I asked Smith if he knew of anyone else who may have had unusual experiences at Williamsburg Hill, and he gave me the name of a resident who has lived on the hill since 2004.

As it turned out, the resident has had several haunting experiences on his property,

My Haunted House on the Hill

Much the same as Smith the hunter, the resident was okay with me using his stories but asked to remain anonymous. So, for the purpose of my interview, I will call him Mr. Jones.

The stories that he told me were chilling and served to add to the strangeness and mystery that has made Williamsburg Hill such a daunting place. A place that has piqued the curiosity of many who live in the region for many years. He not only told stories of ghostly activity that takes place on his property, but offered confirmation of big cats that for years, have been rumored to roam the hill.

"When we first moved to the house in 2004," Jones began. "The nearby land had been hunted for years, so I asked permission to hunt the ground. There was an older gentlemen who went on and on about a black panther in the woods. He claimed that he was once trapped in a tree stand all day by one. I was skeptical about what he told me, because my wife grew up not far from here and her family had talked about black panthers for years, but I had never seen one."

"Needless to say, the next year, I was with my boys up on the hill. When I bought the land, there was a lot of tall grass that I wanted to control, so I threw gasoline on it to burn it off. As soon as I lit it, the noise that was made by whatever screamed at me was un-real! My boys, who were ages four and five at the time, were on the right-hand side of me and they could see in the grass better than me. All of a sudden, they started screaming, (big kitty, big kitty,) and took off running down the hill to the house. I didn't see anything, but I'm thinking when I lit the gasoline, it scared whatever it was off. After that, I started thinking, maybe there is something to all the stories about big cats on the hill. Because that scream was loud and chilling!"

"At the time, we were raising LaMancha goats, and they weighed about eighty pounds each. We had two of them and they both disappeared the same night. The goats were corralled by a six-foot white fence, and whatever took them, jumped over the fence with them. A coyote might make it three or four feet over a fence but would not be able to jump over a six-foot fence with an eighty-pound goat in its mouth."

I asked Mr. Jones if he found any tracks and he said he didn't find tracks or any evidence of what took them, as the ground was frozen.

"In 2006, I had a friend coming to the house," Jones said.

"The road curves near my house, and when the friend arrived, he came running in the house all excited, saying that he just saw a black panther. My Dad was over that night, so we went outside. The noise this thing made was unreal! It made you stop in your tracks and was nothing like I had ever heard before," Jones exclaimed.

"We just started raising goats again this year, because it took me that long to get over it, because I couldn't explain what happened to the goats that disappeared."

I asked Jones if he had ever found big cat tracks while hunting, and he told me that he has not nor has he caught them on the deer cameras that he has set up in the woods. He has recorded bobcats on camera and has seen them in his yard, but never big cats. Jones told me that the big cat type activity has subsided since 2006 and he has not heard or seen any signs of them since then.

"My kids are eighteen and nineteen now, and they still remember the experience they had seeing and hearing the big cat scream. It's something they will never forget."

After discussing Jones's experiences with big cat's our conversation turned to his encounters with the paranormal which he and his family have witnessed both in the house and garage.

Jones started out by telling me about a strange incident that he and his Dad witnessed that took place in the garage.

"There are several deer cams in my garage that I monitor," he began. "On the night in question, Dad and I were watching them. Also, in the garage, there is a sixty-pound heavy bag, like you would use for boxing training. The bag was attached by four cables, one on each corner of the bag, top and bottom, so it would move when hit, but the cables helped to stabilize the bag. Dad and I were sitting at a table eating supper, when all of a sudden, the punching bag went straight up in the air on its own and almost hit the ceiling. It came down and stopped on a dime with no movement whatsoever. Neither Dad nor I could figure out what happened. We sat there looking at each other dumbfounded because we didn't know what to say."

Jones and his Dad tried to recreate what happened, but try as they may, could not get the bag to bounce as high as it did on its own.

"Several times when the boys were younger, they also witnessed the punching bag move on its own and we couldn't figure it out then either," he added.

Jones went on to tell me a story about the first time that his wife's cousin visited their house.

"It was in the summer and my wife's cousin was inside using the bathroom. Everyone else was outside. As he was sitting on the toilet, out of the blue, the doorknob started to rattle and turn. So, he called out, (Hey, real funny guys,) but the rattling continued for a bit then finally stopped. When he came outside and explained what happened, we told him that no one was inside the house, except for him."

Jones told me that since the incident, the same thing has happened to several other people visiting the house and it's always when they are in the house alone, that the doorknob starts moving.

I asked Jones if the jiggling of the doorknob was violent and he said it was not. *"The doorknob twist and turns like someone is trying to get in,"* he explained.

This is where the story gets even more interesting. Jones told me that several other people have lived in his house before he bought the property, including a man who lived in the house sometime back in the late sixties or early seventies that was said to have been involved in Satanic rituals.

"We were told when we moved in that the people who originally lived in the house were involved in Satanic rituals and animal mutilations. We were also told that when a previous owner remodeled the house, he found shackles in the doorways, and a Pegasus showerhead, and a two-way mirror in the shower. Supposedly they buried barrels on the property with who knows what in them and conducted Satanic worshiping, really weird stuff."

I asked Jones if he thought the mutilated cattle that were found were connected to the rituals.

"I think so," he said. "The newspaper article I saw about the mutilations were labeled as UFO related. From what I gathered from the article, the cows were laying on their sides and were drained of their blood, with no puncture wounds. The cattle were found in a pasture, just east of our house. But what happened to the cattle is a mystery."

"We were told about all the weird stuff that supposedly went on in the house the first year we moved in. Since then we have heard voices in the house, and we hear them all the time. My wife and I can be at one end of the house and the boys gone, and we will hear voices. At one time a paranormal group from Mattoon, investigated the house, and they recorded a child's laughter."

Jones told me that so far, the activity in the house, although strange, has been benign in nature. *"It's like someone is here,"* he said.

He then told me of another ghostly incident they have witnessed.

"One time we were having a family gathering and had tables set up outside in front of our kitchen window. Everyone was seated at the tables, when a man, inside the house, walked in front of the window, looked at us and kept going. We all saw him!"

Based on my interviews with Scott Turley, Mr. Smith, and Mr. Jones. It becomes clearer that the strangeness that takes place at Williamsburg Hill is not limited to the graveyard but encompasses the hill itself. Which raises the question, is the activity in the woods a byproduct of what goes on in the graveyard or is the activity in the graveyard the result of something about the land it sits on.

The abundance of limestone has long been associated with paranormal activity, and through my research I have found that Williamsburg Hill is basically a mound of limestone covered by a layer of topsoil.

No one is really sure why locations that have a superabundance of limestone seem to have an equal abundance of paranormal activity. Some believe it has something to do with quartz in the limestone that serves to alter or magnify energy frequencies that either allow us to experience things that we may normally not be able to sense or allows ghost and beings from other realms, access to our world. Of course, neither of these theories has been proven, only speculated.

I can say, however, that in my twenty years of investigating the paranormal, locations with an abundance of limestone, seem to have more reports of paranormal activity than locations that don't.

For example, cities like, Alton and Quincy, Illinois, Hannibal, Missouri and Atchison, Kansas are all cities where large amounts of limestone exist and if you asked the folks who live in these cities to name the homes and businesses that are haunted, they would tell you it would be easier to give you a list of the ones that are not.

Whether it be limestone, supernatural portals, interdimensional windows, or some other unknown force that is the catalyst causing the strange activity taking place on Williamsburg Hill, remains secondary to the wide array of unexplained activity witnessed by residents and visitors to the hill for many years.

Making Williamsburg Hill unique when compared to other haunted locations is the varietal paranormal stew of ghosts, ghouls and phantoms that have been witnessed and let us not forget to add to the pot, strange lights, cattle mutilations and voices from nowhere.

Based on what I have witnessed, and others have told me, the unexplained activity that makes Williamsburg Hill so strange, is showing no signs of slowing down, and the final curtain on those residing in Ridge Cemetery, may not be so final after all!

Epilogue

"And I saw a ghost wandering under the fading trees, still clinging to life; tired of earth, unready for heaven. I heard the quiet feet of a ghost stirring the fallen leaves, and a sigh echoing the sighing in the stripped branches."
~Dallas Kenmare Browne Kelsey

I have always been fascinated by mysteries. To me these perplexities of nature, especially those that contain an element of the extraordinary, are as intoxicating as downing a bottle of your favorite wine. An odd occurrence: a mysterious stranger who appears out of nowhere; missing time, missing people, psychic visions, cryptid creatures, ghost, ghouls, and goblins to name a few.

These wonders are embedded in the fabric of the universe, whose door, if left open, offers a glimpse into the unknown.

Williamsburg Hill's Ridge Cemetery is a place where many of the things I mentioned are witnessed regularly. But why? What is it about the hill that attracts such an array of strangeness?

There seems to be an invisible world with its own cast of characters waiting for the right moment to intermingle with complete strangers.

After investigating the unexplained for over two decades, I can say with certainty, there is a world beyond ours, where things once here and things we can only imagine, exist. Somehow Williamsburg Hills Ridge Cemetery provides a home to such things.

Over the years, many have ventured to the hill hoping to be entertained by the phantoms and monsters who dwell in the graveyard and surrounding woods. Based on things I have witnessed, and stories told to me by others, rather than being spectators, we are more likely the entertainment.

Who or whatever was in the woods the night I encountered the whistling seemed to be surreptitiously stalking me. It could move about freely following my every move without making a sound, at one point coming as close as ten feet from me.

I don't know of anyone or anything capable of moving around in a pitch-black woods, in silence or without using some type of light, but whatever it was, did.

Nor do I know of anyone or anything capable of covertly transporting a heavy-duty lawn tractor from the center of a graveyard, place it unscathed in the nearby woods and the owner who is close by, hears nothing.

Equally strange are the logs and trees that mysteriously appear across the road, blocking the exit of unsuspecting visitors to the graveyard. Like the tractor vanishing and re-appearing in the woods, the logs suddenly appear, and nothing is heard.

Stories of an old man searching for bars, and a woman in black looking for a playmate for children she claims are under the ground, are the type of stories that nightmares are made of.

If these things were not strange enough, add to the equation the grave of a young boy, that causes unsuspecting women to become emotional, some to the extent they sob uncontrollably.

Whether by coincidence or if it is somehow linked to the boy's grave, out of the over one-hundred investigations I have conducted at Ridge Cemetery, the only two places I have recorded EVP's in the graveyard is the area next to the Native American graves and recorders placed next to the young boys grave.

Making a list of the strange things I witnessed, and the extraordinary things other eyewitnesses told me about, is no simple task as it is quite long.

Ghosts, unexplained lights in the cemetery, UFO's, large shadowy masses that can leap great distances, barefoot footprints, cattle mutilations, black cloaked figures in the woods, all add to the mystery that is Williamsburg Hill.

Undoubtedly there is something strange taking place, and it is something that has been taking place for years.

You get the sense there is a type of intelligence or consciousness at work there. It is a mixed bag of paranormal strangeness, and a special place that allows you to take a step back in time. A place that is like no other I have investigated and keeps me coming back for more.

What makes Williamsburg Hill so strange, and why has it been a source of so many legends over the years?

Do our minds play tricks on us, or do people actually come into contact with the dead, either by some chance encounter or by laws of nature that we do not understand?

If ghosts exist and hauntings occur, why are some places haunted while others seem normal? Why do some cemeteries feel peaceful, but others, such as Ridge Cemetery, give you the uneasy feeling of being watched and followed?

Do portals and windows exist that allow travel between different dimensions or worlds? If so, who is haunting whom?

Some say they have been to Ridge Cemetery many times and have not experienced the strangeness that so many claim to have encountered. They label the witnesses crazy, and their stories the product of rumors and overactive imaginations.

Unfortunately, this is what many will believe, until they have that chance encounter with the paranormal for themselves. We have been taught to sanitize reality, but in the grand scheme of things, reality is much odder than most are willing to admit.

The next time your daily journey takes you near Tower Hill, exit and turn off the main road. Head down Route 1100 East and check out Ridge Cemetery for yourself.

You never know who or what you might encounter in this odd, but special place. But if you have such an encounter, I assure you, it will be an encounter that you won't soon forget.

Happy Hauntings!

Larry Wilson

Campfire Tales Extra

From the Author

Strange Williamsburg Hill is the second in a series of books called *"Campfire Tales,"* published by Chiller Books.

As an added feature, each book in the *"Campfire Tales"* series includes a section called Paranormal Witness, which allows me to share stories of the encounters of others, as told to me.

Having investigated the unexplained for the last two decades has allowed me to meet some remarkable people. Some of which have become cherished friends.

One such person is Carl Jones, who I not only consider a respected colleague in the field of paranormal research and investigation, but a wonderful friend as well.

So, credit for the chilling story you are about to read goes to Mr. Carl Jones of Auburn, Illinois.

Paranormal Witness

The Antique Trunk

Carl Jones

My name is Carl Jones; I grew up in Springfield, Illinois, near Memorial Hospital. I have been a paranormal investigator since May 1993. The story you are about to read is the reason I began my journey into such an unusual endeavor.

It begins in 1978, on Easter weekend, when one of the worst ice storms on record swept through Central Illinois, bringing freezing temperatures, downed power and telephone lines, power outages and incredible numbers of downed trees and limbs. It even toppled massive television and radio broadcast antennas. The area was devastated by the late March storm.

Earlier in the month we had mild temperatures, teasing us into thinking it would be an early spring. The weather was so nice, that families began having garage sales, which my Dad loved to go to.

Dad enjoyed collecting antiques, and deals could be found at the sales. It was at one such garage sale on the west side of Springfield, near Sacred Heart and Dubois schools, that he found and purchased two antique items.

One was an old vintage Victrola record player with a huge tone arm, and a handle on the side to wind up the player. The other item was a large antique packing trunk. Both were in nice condition.

The trunk looked like a large treasure chest. Inside, the walls of the trunk were lined with flowery wallpaper. There was an insert drawer that lifted out, allowing for additional storage underneath.

My Mom advised Dad not to buy the trunk. She was ok with him buying the old phonograph but had a bad feeling about the trunk and didn't want it.

Despite moms objection, both items ended up coming home with them, as the seller gave Dad an offer he couldn't refuse if he took both items, which he did.

After we brought the antiques home; strange things started happening.

Our house was two-story. The upstairs is where my family lived, and the downstairs was a separate apartment my parents rented out. It had a bedroom, living room, bathroom, and kitchen.

Outside the apartment door and inside a hallway were carpeted steps that led upstairs to our family living space. At the top of the steps was a door. On the other side of the stairs on the lower level, underneath my parent's bedroom, was a small garage that housed Dad's workshop and our washer and dryer.

There was a common entrance at ground level near the garage, used by renters and my family to come and go from the house. As you continue reading, you will see the pertinence of this to the odd happenings.

Prior to the strange things that took place, my parents decided not to rent out the apartment and allowed me to move in, so I could have my own bedroom with more privacy, as I was a teenager and the oldest child. I had three younger brothers who shared a bedroom upstairs.

The garage sale purchases were placed in the downstairs apartment. The Victrola in the kitchen on top of a table, and the trunk placed in the living room atop an antique coffee table, twelve feet from the entrance to the apartment.

The House as it looks today

The first occurrence happened a night or two after we brought the garage sale items home.

It was around midnight and I was sleeping in the downstairs bedroom. I was awakened from a sound sleep by a loud noise that sounded like someone was moving a heavy piece of furniture. From my vantage point, it sounded like it came from upstairs, directly above me.

I jumped up, flipped on the light, and looked around the apartment. Not seeing anything, I went upstairs to see what all the commotion was about. When I opened the upstairs door, my Mom yelled out from her bedroom, *"What in the heck is going on down there, are you moving stuff around?"*

"No," I replied. *"I thought you guys were moving something around up here!"*

Mom explained that they were in bed and hadn't been moving anything. Little did we realize this was only the beginning of the craziness to come.

Not long after the strange noise, the ice storm hit. We were lucky because we didn't lose power for any length of time, since we lived near the hospital and damaged power lines were repaired quicker than in other areas.

One of the first peculiar events we noticed was a handheld hair dryer that turned on by itself.

It would turn on while we were in another room and no one was using it. We would go turn it off, but later, it would turn on by itself again.

This happened often. On one occasion, I shut the hair dryer off and unplugged it from the wall. Later that evening, I heard the hairdryer running. When I went to the bathroom to check it out, no one was in the bathroom and it was plugged in again.

Another time, my aunt came over to spend time with us because her home was without power. She was in the living room talking to my Mom when the hair dryer came on. When they checked it out, no one was in the bathroom.

Late one afternoon, Mom was in her bedroom taking a nap, when she woke up to the sound of the clothes dryer running. The dryer was located under her bedroom. She knew she hadn't turned it on, and nobody else was home.

Mom went downstairs and sure enough, the dryer was running with a few items of clothing in it. She reached inside and noticed that it wasn't even warm, and the dryer typically heated rather quick. She checked the setting, and it was on the hot-dry setting. There was nothing wrong with the dryer, and it worked fine after that.

On another night, Mom and I were watching an old Alfred

Hitchcock film on television with Bette Davis. I don't recall which movie it was, but it was either "Whatever Happened to Baby Jane or Hush Hush Sweet Charlotte." Needless to say, we both were creeped out by the movie.

It was late and Dad was working the night shift, so Mom double checked to make sure the house was closed up and all the doors were securely locked before we went to bed. In the middle of the night, Mom got up to get a drink from the kitchen.

When she passed by the living room, she noticed a strange light illuminating the room. Upon further investigation, she found the front door was open several inches and the streetlight in front of the house was shining into the room.

The door that was open was one she double checked before we went to bed. When she shut the door, she noticed the door was still locked, but the dead bolt lock had been flipped, and somehow had opened with no one else touching it.

The year before the strangeness began, my aunt gave Dad a cool-looking cuckoo clock. It had a deer on it and was patterned in a hunting style motif. She knew Dad would like it being he was an outdoorsman and loved to hunt and fish.

She told us it had never worked because the weighted pendulum that hung beneath the clock and swung back and forth to keep time was missing. All that was there was a piece of metal with a hole in it where the pendulum used to hang.

Dad tried to fashion pendulums for the clock out of wood, plaster, and other materials, but they never worked. So, my parents hung the clock on the living room wall next to the front door, just for looks.

One afternoon I was babysitting my younger brother Matt. We were lounging in the living room watching television, when suddenly we heard, *"cuckoo, cuckoo, cuckoo, cuckoo!"*

We looked at each other like what the heck was that?

I looked at the clock and the little bird was popping in and out the tiny door at the top of the clock, cuckooing like crazy.

The clock had never worked, so we had never heard the sound, nor seen the bird pop out the door before. I walked over to the clock and saw that the piece of metal was swinging back and forth on its own, with no pendulum on it.

The clock was working!

I reached up and stopped the swinging piece of metal to see if it would start up on its own again. Immediately after stopping it, we heard loud rock & roll music coming from the kid's bedroom down the hall.

Heading down the hall to see what was going on, I found that somehow the clock radio sitting on a dresser turned on by itself, and the volume was turned up full blast.

"Maybe the alarm was set to go off at that exact time," I thought to myself. So, I checked to see if the alarm was set, but it wasn't, even though the radio had turned on.

Something had to physically turn the radio on and adjust the volume. It was very unnerving.

When Mom got home, I told her what had happened. She was as perplexed as I was because she knew how hard Dad had tried to get the clock to work.

Later that evening, we were sitting in the living room, and once again, the cuckoo clock started cuckooing and the little bird popped in and out. This time Mom witnessed it as well. As I reached up and stopped the piece of swinging metal, I wondered if the radio would come on again, but it didn't.

Most of the windows in our home had the old type shades

that when you pulled them down, they would lock in place. Now and then a shade would fly up on its own.

One evening I was home alone. All the shades throughout the house were down because it was dark out. I was in the living room reading a book, when suddenly I heard a loud sound that caused the hair to stand up on my neck.

When I checked to see what happened, I found that every shade in the house flew up at the same time. It scared me because you can imagine how loud the noise was. I went from room to room checking the shades and they were all up.

I was too frightened to pull them down for fear that they would fly back up again on their own. So, I turned on the television and turned the volume up and waited for Mom and Dad to come home so I could tell them what happened.

When the weirdness was taking place, I remember how each time I entered the downstairs apartment to go to my bedroom, the front room where the trunk was kept always felt cold. Even in the weeks after the ice storm, when the temperatures had warmed up, it was still cold down there. It felt like we had left a window open, but none were.

Even though I never saw anything, I always felt like I was being watched when downstairs, so much so I slept with a lamp on next to my bed.

It got so bad; I started spending more time upstairs where I felt at ease, especially when the family was around. I dreaded going downstairs at night to go to bed.

One day Mom left to go grocery shopping and run a few errands. When she came home and brought the groceries into the kitchen, something caught her eye.

She glanced over toward the gas range and saw that a burner was on full blast.

There was a frying pan on the burner and when she turned the stove off, she picked it up and noticed it was still cold. This meant the burner had been turned on moments before she walked in the door, but no one else was home. There was definitely something strange going on.

Sometimes when we came home, we would find lights on, that were off when we left, or the television would be on.

During the 1970s we had cable TV, with a push button box that sat on top of the television. You had to get up and push a button to change the station. Several times while watching television; the channel would switch to a different station on its own.

A strange and frightening event took place one evening while I was home with my brother Matt.

We were upstairs in the living room watching television. It was evening right around sundown, when we heard a weird knocking on the window next to our front door. It was a thud type knock.

I looked up but didn't see anyone through the window. But we both heard it, it was a *"knock, knock, knock."*

Thinking it was an ornery neighborhood kid named James playing a prank, I jumped up and went to the door, quickly opened it, to catch him in the act. But no one was there.

Moments later I heard the same knock, knock, knock, only this time, it was coming from my Mom and Dad's bedroom down the hall. Their bedroom had two windows, one facing the front of the house, and one facing the east.

Who or whatever it was, rapped three times on their front window, then moved to the side window and knocked three times again.

It was so loud; I could see the window vibrating with each knock. It was the same, *"knock, knock, knock!"*

Even though it was getting dark out, I could see through the window and there was no one there.

The frightening thing about it, to reach the windows, you needed a ladder, because they were second-floor windows, and couldn't be reached from the ground level.

The knocking continued, moving from window to window in a clockwise manner around the house.

Next, it moved to the window in my brother's room. *"Knock, knock, knock,"* again violently rattling the window with each knock. The knocking then moved to the window that overlooked our backyard at the rear of the house, then to the bathroom window, the two kitchen windows, and finally to the living room window on the west side of our house.

Someone or something knocked on every window of the second story of our house. Eventually stopping at the window, the knocking began. You can imagine how frightening this was.

As a sixteen-year-old teenager, and having my own bedroom downstairs, my main entertainment was my stereo. I spent countless hours in my room listening to the radio, playing records, and reading.

Several times, when I came home from school, and walked into my room, I would find my stereo or the overhead light turned on, and I knew I had turned them off before leaving. Other times the bathroom or kitchen light would be on.

Much of the strangeness was experienced by my Mom, who was home alone during the day while my brother's and I were at school and Dad was at work.

She noticed things that caused her to ask questions of herself, like, *"Did I turn this or that on and forget to turn it off?"*

Being alone during the day, Mom felt uneasy by all the strange things taking place, wondering what would be next.

We had lived in the house for years, and nothing like the strangeness we were experiencing happened before Dad purchased the antiques and brought them into our home.

Mom and I tried telling Dad about the strange things going on, but he thought we were over-reacting and watching too many scary films on television. In fairness, Dad was at work when much of what took place happened, so he missed out on the odd events that were taking place.

Although Dad was skeptical when it came to ghost and the paranormal, he too experienced some of the strangeness for himself.

One day while downstairs he noticed someone had been messing with the old Victrola record player. The tone arm had been moved to the middle of the player, and some of the stylus needles were scattered around it. Even some of the screws had been loosened or removed.

He also noticed that someone had been messing with an old-fashioned antique telephone downstairs as well. This upset Dad and he blamed us kids for playing with it, even though we knew better than to touch Dad's things.

We told him it wasn't us, and I think it was at this point that he started believing some of the stories of the strange activity going on in the house we had been telling him.

One afternoon, Dad was taking a shower getting ready for work. Mom was in the kitchen fixing a meal for him to take with him. Suddenly they both heard heavy footsteps on the stairwell that lead downstairs.

The steps were carpeted, so for my parents to hear them, meant either someone was walking heavily or stomping their feet. In fact, the footsteps were so heavy that Dad could hear and feel the vibration from them, even with the door to the bathroom closed.

We rarely used the door at the top of the steps, so it was never opened, and as far as they knew, nobody came in.

Dad walked out of the bathroom as Mom was coming down the hall with the meal she had packed for him. When she heard the footsteps, she thought Dad was leaving without the food she prepared.

Looking at each other, they both asked, *"Who in the world was stomping on the stairs?"* At first they thought it was the other, since they knew my brother's and I were at school and nobody else was home. When they realized it wasn't, they became alarmed.

Dad opened the door to the stairwell and went down the steps to investigate. He searched the entire downstairs and found nothing. The lower level door to the outside was locked, and the apartment door was shut.

More and more, the strange things that were happening frightened Mom. She wondered why all the peculiar things were happening to us. My youngest brothers were too young to notice the strangeness, but my brother Matt and I were as perplexed and frightened as Mom. Even Dad was starting to wonder what was going on.

One day my Mom was talking to a neighbor on the telephone and told her about some of the things we had been experiencing. The lady asked Mom, *"Have you brought anything new into the house recently?"*

This got my Mom thinking. She remembered that other than groceries, the only things we had brought in, were the antique items from the garage sale.

Call it mother's intuition or a sixth sense, Mom instinctively knew it had to be the old trunk. The one she had told Dad that she didn't want because it gave her a bad feeling.

My Mom has always had a certain clairvoyance about things and places, and she knew she didn't want the trunk when she laid eyes on it. Even before Dad brought it home, it made her uncomfortable. Something from within was telling her that the strangeness was originating from the trunk.

When Dad came home from work that evening, Mom told him she was not spending another night in the house, unless he removed the trunk.

Not having any place to take it, he put it in the front yard, near the street.

The weather was much warmer, and rain wasn't expected for a few days, so that's where the trunk sat for several nights. Nothing unusual happened during the time it sat in the front yard.

But, haunted or not, Dad knew he couldn't leave the trunk sitting outside for long, because eventually it would rain, and he didn't want to ruin an antique piece of furniture.

So, he took it to his Mom and Dad's house and put it in their detached garage next to their house.

My Grandmother told us that during the time it was in their garage, they heard noises, like things were being moved around, and clinking and clanging sounds as though tools were being jostled about. Several times, they found the garage light on when nobody had been out there.

Our house returned to normal and nothing unusual happened after the trunk was removed.

A week after Dad took the trunk to my Grandparents, he brought it back to our house and again put it in the front yard.

Then, one day, Dad told the story about the trunk to some of his work buddies. One co-worker knew a young couple who collected antiques, so he told them about it, and they said they would like to have the trunk. The co-worker told the couple about what happened to us, but they still wanted it.

They told Dad's friend they didn't believe in ghost and hauntings and found the stories a bit humorous. Besides, my Dad was giving it to them for free, so they wanted it.

Later that day a truck pulled up with the man and woman and their two young children, a girl, and a boy. They drove away with the trunk, and that was the last we saw of it, thank goodness! But it wasn't the last we heard of it, oh no.

A few days later, Dad's buddy came to work and said to him, *"Hey, do you remember the folks who came and picked up your old trunk?"*

"Yes!" Dad replied.

"Well, they took it home with them and placed it downstairs in the basement area. Last night, just after dusk, they decided to go to Dairy Queen for some ice cream. They turned off the lights, locked up the house, hopped into their car and were backing out of the driveway when they saw the lights turn on inside of their home."

A few days later, Dad's same buddy came to work and said, *"You know that family that got your trunk?"*

"Yep," Dad replied. *"What happened?"*

"Well, the other night around 11:30 P.M. or so, the family had just slipped into their beds and were relaxing when they heard loud footsteps coming up from the basement."

Fortunately, that was the last that we ever heard of the trunk. So, I am not sure if the family who bought it had any further experiences or not.

The haunting my family experienced in the 1970s sparked my interest in the paranormal, so much so, that I have read hundreds of books on ghosts, hauntings, UFO's, Cryptids and just about anything related to the paranormal I can get my hands on.

In addition, I became a paranormal investigator and have been on countless investigations, having had some interesting experiences, all in a quest to find answers to why these things happened.

I moderate a monthly discussion group about the paranormal and teach a class about it at Lincoln Land Community College in Springfield, Illinois.

On one occasion, I took one of my classes on an investigation to the oldest home in Springfield. As we were doing the initial walkthrough, I noticed a small room at the top of the stairs, where I found five or six trunks identical to the one that my Dad bought at the garage sale.

Needless to say, this shocked me and made my heart skip a beat or two and I may have whispered an expletive under my breath.

I went downstairs and asked the woman who was our host if she knew anything about the trunks.

She told me that some came from the Ursuline nuns convent and presumed the others came from another convent or men's monastery. She said the trunks were given to men and women entering a convent or monastery and were used to store belongings they wanted to keep for their earthly existence, while they gave everything else up for God.

I have often pondered why an old packing trunk would be haunted.

Perhaps the answer lies in what the host told me.

If the worldly belongings that meant everything to them were placed into a trunk, is it possible that even after death, the former owner of the trunk followed it wherever it went?

Or perhaps there is a darker, more sinister reason. Unfortunately, we may never know the answer. So, a word of caution to those who are reading this.

Please be very careful what you bring into your home. Because some things really are haunted.

ABOUT THE AUTHOR

Larry Wilson spent a decade working as a private investigator, before turning his attention to the paranormal. He is the founder of Urban Paranormal Investigations in Central Illinois.

In addition to investigating hundreds of locations throughout the Midwest, he is a "Best-Selling Author" who has written several books on the topic, guest lecturer, and has appeared on both television and radio programs.

He is founder of 11:11 Films, an independent film company that produces paranormal documentaries. Larry has also assisted in the filming of three paranormal documentaries for other independent film companies.

Wilson resides in Taylorville, Illinois with his wife Kathy.

For more information, please visit:
http://lwilsonurbanparanormalblogspot.com/

Like us on Facebook:
https://www.facebook.com/Urban-Paranormal-Investigations-327088597440791/

Photo by Kathy Wilson

Books by Larry Wilson

Chasing Shadows
Echoes from the Grave
Dark Creepy Places
Where Evil Lurks
Dr. Ugs
Paranormal Road Trip
Strange Williamsburg Hill

www.ingramcontent.com/pod-product-compliance
Lightning Source LLC
LaVergne TN
LVHW051606070426
835507LV00021B/2797